The 10-Step Solution for a Stress-Free Retirement

EMILY BRANDON
Senior Editor for Retirement,
U.S. News & World Report

adamsmedia

Avon, Massachusetts

Published by
Adams Media, a division of F+W Media, Inc.
57 Littlefield Street, Avon, MA 02322. U.S.A.
www.adamsmedia.com

ISBN 10: 1-4405-9075-3
ISBN 13: 978-1-4405-9075-7
eISBN 10: 1-4405-9076-1
eISBN 13: 978-1-4405-9076-4

Printed in the United States of America.

10   9   8   7   6   5   4   3   2   1

Many of the designations used by manufacturers and sellers to distinguish their products are claimed as trademarks. Where those designations appear in this book and F+W Media, Inc. was aware of a trademark claim, the designations have been printed with initial capital letters.

This publication is designed to provide accurate and authoritative information with regard to the subject matter covered. It is sold with the understanding that the publisher is not engaged in rendering legal, accounting, or other professional advice. If legal advice or other expert assistance is required, the services of a competent professional person should be sought.
—From a *Declaration of Principles* jointly adopted by a Committee of the American Bar Association and a Committee of Publishers and Associations

Cover design by Erin Alexander.
Cover illustrations by Kathy Konkle.

This book is available at quantity discounts for bulk purchases.
For information, please call 1-800-289-0963.

Dedication

To Charlotte and Peter

CONTENTS

INTRODUCTION

Most of us want to eventually stop working and begin enjoying a well-deserved retirement. The problem lies in how to pay for it. We typically have enough trouble covering our monthly bills, let alone funding a twenty- or thirty-year period of leisure. In years past, our employers helped solve the problem. Many companies provided a pension that offered a significant source of income during retirement. Today, that's seldom the case. Most employers no longer offer traditional pension plans, which is a major change from the generation who came before us. In place of these vanished pensions, we must piece together a retirement income from a variety of sources. Our retirement plan is built out of a combination of Social Security, Medicare, and money saved for retirement, typically in a 401(k) or IRA.

The Golden Age of Pensions

It wasn't always this way. In 1980, about 39 percent of the labor force had a traditional pension plan, according to Department of Labor data. The number of traditional pension plans peaked in 1983 at more than 175,000. These pensions provided retirement security for millions of workers. With a pension plan, once you meet the appropriate age and number of years on the job, you can retire knowing that your former employer will provide you monthly payments from your retirement date onward. In most cases, these payments continue for the rest of your life.

While less than half of workers were ever fortunate enough to have a pension, those who did have one could retire with a steady stream of monthly payments in addition to Social Security and their personal savings. The plan sponsor often hired an investment expert to manage plan assets, and no investment knowledge on the part of the employee was required. The federal government even insured most private-sector pension plans and paid out benefits up to certain annual limits if the plan failed.

Alas, few of us today will ever experience the retirement security such pensions provide. The proportion of people with traditional pensions has fallen relentlessly since 1980. By 2012 there were fewer than 44,000 traditional pension plans left, and the number has continued to drop. Almost all of us are now pensionless. In their place, the 401(k) plan has risen as the new predominant workplace retirement benefit. As of 2015 some 61 percent of private industry workers had the option to participate in a 401(k) plan or similar type of workplace retirement account. However, only 43 percent of employees actually used the plan.

401(k)s: The New Retirement Standard

In contrast to pension plans, you bear nearly all of the risk associated with your 401(k) plan, and your ability to retire comfortably suffers if you underuse the account. You and your employer must each decide how much to deposit in the account. You must also select investments that will build wealth for the future while also avoiding losses. Often the only investment training you will receive is a one-hour seminar provided by the 401(k) plan sponsor about how the account works.

The benefits of a 401(k) plan depend on your ability to save consistently, invest prudently, and make it through a gauntlet of fees and penalties. When you change jobs or retire, you will also need to familiarize yourself with individual retirement accounts to maintain the tax benefits of your 401(k) plan. How well you are able to use these retirement accounts, and avoid the taxes and penalties associated with them, will ultimately determine your retirement lifestyle.

Using What You've Got

While you may never receive a traditional pension from a former employer, there is a lot you can do to make the best of the retirement benefits you do have. This book will walk you through ten steps that will improve your retirement finances. You can boost your financial situation, even on the verge of retirement, by strategically securing more money from Social Security and getting your employer to help pay for retirement. There are also a variety of tax deductions and credits available to retirement savers that can help you grow your money faster.

Retirement planning problems often arise when you don't know all the rules and conditions associated with the various types of retirement benefits. Many retirement benefits have both age-related and calendar-year deadlines, and the penalties for missing them can be severe. It's important to know how to avoid surcharges on your Medicare benefits and fees on your 401(k) and many other rules and gotchas that have the potential to trip you up as you prepare for retirement. Successfully avoiding fees and penalties can help you minimize costs and boost the value of your retirement benefits.

Your retirement security depends on your ability to use each type of retirement benefit. Those who know how to get more money from Social Security and pay less in taxes may be able to enjoy a higher retirement income than people who are unfamiliar with these strategies. It's worth the time to learn how to make optimum use of your retirement benefits. The deck is stacked against you, but you can still play your best hand.

STEP 1
MAXIMIZE SOCIAL SECURITY

Social Security is the foundation on which your retirement finances are built. Most people pay into the system beginning with their first paycheck and begin to collect payments in their sixties. Benefits are calculated based on the amount you have paid in and when you choose to start receiving benefits (*www.ssa.gov/retire/apply.html*).

Though the benefits are typically modest, they are an important source of retirement income because they are guaranteed to last for the rest of your life no matter how long you live. Furthermore, they are adjusted for inflation each year, so they won't lose value over time. For many people, and especially those facing retirement without traditional pensions, Social Security is the only source of retirement income that provides these guarantees.

The vast majority of those who are retired (86 percent) receive income from Social Security. The program provides at least half of the retirement income of 65 percent of retirees, and more than a third receive 90 percent or more of their retirement income from Social Security payments.

In 2014 the average Social Security payment to retired workers was $1,294 per month—a big jump from the payout to Ida May Fuller (the first recipient of Social Security), but still small relative to today's living expenses. Retired couples in 2014 received an average of

$2,111. However, this payment varies considerably by individual and is significantly influenced by three important factors:

1. How much you earn and contribute to Social Security while working
2. The number of years you work
3. The age at which you sign up for Social Security

There are a variety of ways to increase the amount you get from Social Security each month, and in this step we'll examine them in detail. Here is how to boost the payments you will receive from Social Security in retirement.

The Origins of Social Security

The Social Security program was created in 1935 by President Franklin Roosevelt. Workers began to pay into the system in 1937, and monthly benefits were distributed starting in 1940. The initial contribution amount was 1 percent. The payroll tax has been gradually increased over several decades, first hitting 3 percent in 1960 and 5 percent in 1978. The current tax rate of 6.2 percent has been in effect since 1990. The original Social Security Act promised benefit payments that ranged from $10 to $85 per month. The first monthly retirement payment was issued to sixty-five-year-old Ida May Fuller of Ludlow, Vermont, for $22.54. During Fuller's lifetime Social Security payments to retirees could be increased only by special acts of Congress. Automatic cost-of-living adjustments for retirees were added to the Social Security program in 1972 and paid out beginning in 1975.

Maximize Your Earnings

The first way to boost your Social Security payments begins while you are still working. Employees pay 6.2 percent of their earnings into the Social Security system, and employers pay a matching 6.2 percent. Self-employed workers pay in 12.4 percent of their earnings. This payroll tax applies only to money earned up to a limit, which was $118,500 in 2016. Earnings above $118,500 are not taxed by Social Security or used to calculate Social Security benefits. However, the more you earn and pay into Social Security up to the limit, the bigger your payments will be in retirement.

It's particularly important to pay into Social Security for at least thirty-five years. Social Security payments are calculated based on the thirty-five years in which you earn the most. If you haven't worked for thirty-five years, zeros are averaged into the calculation for the years you didn't work, which can significantly lower your retirement payout. If you work for more than thirty-five years, each higher-earning year will cancel out a lower-earning year in the benefit calculation. So aim to *pay into Social Security for at least thirty-five years.*

Select Your Start Date

Even if you are already on the verge of retirement, it's not too late to boost your Social Security payments. The age you start Social Security benefits plays a big role in how much your monthly payments will be.

Workers are eligible to begin receiving Social Security payments at age sixty-two, but monthly payments are significantly reduced if you sign up at this age. To receive the full amount you have earned, you need to claim Social Security at your full retirement age, which is typically sixty-six or sixty-seven. The full retirement age for those whose birth year is 1937 or earlier was sixty-five, but it has been raised for everyone born after that.

The full retirement age increases in two-month increments from sixty-five and two months for those born in 1938 to sixty-five and ten months for people born in 1942. The full retirement age is sixty-six for everyone born between 1943 and 1954. The age workers can claim full benefits then increases two months each year from sixty-six and two months for baby boomers born in 1955 to sixty-six and ten months for those born in 1959. The full retirement age is sixty-seven for everyone born in 1960 or later.

Important Social Security Ages

The age at which you sign up for Social Security impacts the size of your monthly payments. Here are the key ages to pay attention to:

- **Age Sixty-Two.** This is the earliest possible age you can sign up for benefits, but monthly payments are reduced if you claim payments at this age.
- **Age Sixty-Five.** People born in 1937 or earlier are eligible for their full Social Security benefit at age sixty-five. The full retirement age is sixty-five and two months for people born in 1938 and increases by two months for each year after that until reaching sixty-five and ten months for people born in 1942.
- **Age Sixty-Six.** The full retirement age is sixty-six for most baby boomers born between 1943 and 1954. The full retirement age then increases by two months per year from sixty-six and two months for those born in 1955 to sixty-six and ten months for people born in 1959. Once you turn your full retirement age, you can also work and claim Social Security benefits without having part or all of your payments withheld.
- **Age Sixty-Seven.** Everyone born in 1960 or later can begin to claim unreduced Social Security benefits at age sixty-seven.
- **Age Seventy.** Social Security payments will increase by about 8 percent per year if you delay claiming benefits until age seventy. After you reach seventy, there is no additional benefit to waiting to sign up for Social Security benefits.

In addition to knowing about these ages, there are two additional points that are important to keep in mind as you consider how to maximize your Social Security payouts.

Benefits Are Reduced for Early Claiming

If you sign up for Social Security benefits before your full retirement age, your benefits will be reduced, depending on how early you claim. A worker born in 1965 who signs up for Social Security at age sixty-two will receive 30 percent smaller payments than if he waited until age sixty-seven to claim. For example, a worker who would be eligible for $1,680 a month at age sixty-seven would get just $1,159 monthly at age sixty-two.

FOR EXAMPLE

After paying in 6.2 percent of every paycheck for thirty-five years, John is eager to sign up for Social Security payments. He's checked his Social Security statement and knows that he will be eligible for payments worth $1,000 per month at age sixty-six, his full retirement age. But he has lots of bills to pay, and he can't resist the temptation to claim payments now. Instead of waiting until his full retirement age, he signs up for reduced payments of $750 per month beginning at age sixty-two.

Bill is also eligible for payments worth $1,000 per month at age sixty-six, and like John he has a lot of bills to pay. However, he is interested in getting the highest possible monthly Social Security payment. He decides to delay claiming payments until age seventy, after he accrues four years of delayed retirement credits and qualifies for payments worth $1,320 per month. While it's tough for Bill to go without Social Security payments in his sixties, to him it's worth it to wait for a higher benefit payment in his seventies and eighties.

John will receive smaller payments over a longer period of time, while Bill will receive much larger payments later in retirement. Who will come out ahead over his lifetime depends on how long they live. If they both live to be eighty-five, John will have received $207,000 from Social Security over his lifetime, while Bill will have gotten $237,600, or $30,600 more. And if they both live to be ninety-five, Bill comes out $99,000 ahead, not counting his cost-of-living adjustments. However, if they pass at age seventy-five, John, who has been claiming payments for thirteen years, comes out $79,200 ahead of Bill, who was only able to claim five years of larger payments.

Payments Can Be Increased by Later Claiming

If you delay signing up for Social Security after your full retirement age, your payments will increase by 8 percent per year up until age seventy. A worker eligible for $1,680 a month at age sixty-seven could boost his payments to $2,094 each month if he waited until age seventy to claim payments. After age seventy, payments do not further increase due to delayed claiming.

These higher payments last for the rest of your life, no matter how long you live. Social Security payments are also adjusted to keep up with inflation each year. The higher your initial monthly payment, the bigger the dollar value of your inflation adjustments. For example, a worker who claimed payments of $1,159 monthly at age sixty-two would get about $17 more after a 1.5 percent inflation adjustment. But a worker who receives $2,094 each month due to signing up for Social Security at age seventy would get $31 more from the same inflation adjustment.

Buyer's Remorse

If you sign up for Social Security early and then later change your mind about taking the reduced payments, you have a couple of options to increase your benefit. If you signed up for Social Security less than twelve months ago, you can pay back all the money you have received, without interest, and withdraw your Social Security application. This allows you to re-apply for Social Security at a future date and get higher payments. However, if you have been receiving payments from Social Security for a year or more, you're no longer eligible to pay back the money and start over. Furthermore, each beneficiary is only allowed to withdraw his or her Social Security application once.

Inflation Adjustments

Social Security payments are adjusted each year to keep up with inflation as measured by the Consumer Price Index for Urban Wage Earners and Clerical Workers. Cost-of-living adjustments have ranged from 0 in 2010, 2011, and 2016 to 14.3 percent in 1980. The 1.7 percent cost-of-living adjustment in 2015 resulted in the typical retiree getting about $22 more per month.

Another option if you are full retirement age or older is to suspend your retirement benefit payments going forward and then restart them at another time at a higher rate. While this strategy does not completely undo early claiming, it allows you to accrue delayed retirement credits and increase your later payments by 8 percent for each year your payments are suspended. It typically takes a month for a payment suspension to go into effect, so if you request a benefit suspension in July, you will still receive an August payment. You can request that the payments be restarted at any time. Unless you make another election, your payments will automatically restart at age seventy. It's important to note that, beginning in May 2016, suspending your Social Security benefit will also suspend payments that your spouse or other dependents receive based on your work record. Also, if your Medicare Part B premium was deducted from your Social Security checks, you will get a bill for the premium if you suspend your payments.

FOR EXAMPLE

Sam signed up for a reduced Social Security payment of $700 per month at age sixty-two. He would like to increase his Social Security payments and has enough in savings to pay his bills for four years. At age sixty-six he decides to suspend his Social Security payments so that he can earn delayed retirement credits of 8 percent per year and get a bigger retirement benefit later on in retirement. By suspending his payments for four years, he gives up payments of $33,600. However, when his benefit automatically resumes at age seventy, his monthly payments will be 32 percent higher and total $924 per month. (It could actually be a little higher than this due to cost-of-living adjustments.) These higher benefit payments will last the rest of his life. When Sam passes away, his wife Susan will inherit the larger monthly payments.

When deciding the optimal age to sign up for Social Security, it helps to think about how long you expect to live. A man who turns sixty-five in 2016 can expect to live about another 19.5 years until age eighty-four. The life expectancy for a woman the same age is eighty-seven, according to Social Security Administration estimates (*www.socialsecurity.gov/OACT/population/longevity.html*). If you are in poor health or have a reason to believe that you won't live a long life, it can make sense to sign up for Social Security earlier. (However, some people who are in failing health might want to think about taking steps to increase their benefit so a surviving spouse can inherit it.) But if your parents and grandparents lived into their nineties and you have no serious health problems, you will get bigger payments later on in retirement if you delay claiming Social Security.

Coordinate Benefits with a Spouse

If you're married, you can use additional Social Security claiming strategies to maximize your payments as a couple. People who are married are eligible to claim benefits based on their own work record or up to 50 percent of their spouse's benefit, whichever is higher.

To claim the 50 percent spousal payment, the lower-earning or nonworking spouse needs to sign up for spousal payments at his or her full retirement age, which is sixty-six for most baby boomers. Just like individual benefits, spousal benefits are reduced if you claim them before your full retirement age. If you sign up for spousal payments early you will get 32.5 percent of the higher earner's benefit at age sixty-two and 41.7 percent at age sixty-five, instead of the 50 percent you will get if you sign up at your full retirement age.

Married couples who turned sixty-two in 2015 or an earlier year can use another claiming strategy to boost their benefit as a couple. Some married couples can even claim Social Security benefits twice, first as a spouse, and then later based on their own work record. Dual-earner couples who have reached their full retirement age can claim

FOR EXAMPLE

Melissa earns a Social Security benefit of $1,600 per month. Her husband, Mike, who didn't work during their marriage, is eligible for a maximum possible Social Security spousal payment of half that amount ($800) when he reaches his full retirement age. However, Mike decides to claim his spousal payments three years before his full retirement age at sixty-three. As a result, Mike's payment is reduced to 37.5 percent of his wife's benefit and he receives $600 per month, $200 less than he would have gotten if he'd waited until he was sixty-six.

spousal benefits and then later switch to payments based on their own work record, which will then be higher due to delayed claiming. For example, a baby boomer wife could sign up for spousal payments worth 50 percent of her husband's benefit at age sixty-six and then switch to benefits based on her own work record at age seventy. This gets the couple four years of spousal payments and then higher benefit payments later in retirement because they've started payments at an older age. However, only one member of a married couple can receive spouse's benefits and delay his or her own retirement benefits until a later date. The Bipartisan Budget Act of 2015 discontinued the ability to use this Social Security claiming strategy. So, workers who turn sixty-two in 2016 or any later year will no longer be able to claim these two types of payments at different times, but must choose whichever is higher.

You can also claim Social Security benefits based on an ex-spouse's work record if the marriage lasted at least ten years. You might need to provide your marriage certificate and divorce decree to verify the dates. Former spouses can claim as much as 50 percent of the worker's benefit if they sign up for payments at their full retirement age. Like married couples, the percentage is reduced if you claim payments before your full retirement age. Even if your ex-spouse has not yet signed up for benefits, a former spouse can still claim payments if the divorce has lasted for at least two years. The amount of benefits a former spouse receives has no effect on the payments for which the worker or a new spouse is eligible. However, if a divorced spouse remarries, he or she generally cannot collect benefits based on an ex-spouse's work record unless the marriage ends.

Maximize Survivor's Benefits

When one member of a retired married couple dies, the surviving spouse gets whichever member of the couple's Social Security payments is higher. So, if a husband gets $1,500 per month from Social Security and his wife receives $1,200 per month, the wife would be paid $1,500 per month after her husband dies because her husband's payments were higher than hers. The higher earner can maximize the benefit the surviving spouse will receive by delaying claiming Social Security as long as possible up until age seventy. Conversely, when a member of a married couple claims retirement benefits early, he or she is also reducing the amount the surviving spouse will receive.

A widow or widower who is full retirement age or older typically receives 100 percent of the higher earner's benefit. You can start collecting survivor's payments as early as age sixty, but the benefit payments are reduced a fraction of a percent for each month you claim before full retirement age. Spouses who claim survivor's payments before their full retirement age typically get between 71 and 99 percent of the deceased spouse's payments. For example, for a baby boomer woman whose full retirement age is sixty-six, a survivor's benefit of $1,000 would be reduced to $810 if she begins claiming at age sixty-two.

A person who receives survivor's benefits can later switch to his or her own retirement benefit if it's higher. A widow who signed up for survivor's benefits early at age sixty-two could switch to her own full retirement benefit at age sixty-six. There is also a one-time payment of $255 that Social Security can make to a spouse or child if he or she applies for this payment within two years of the date of death.

You typically cannot claim widow's or widower's benefits if you remarry before age sixty, but you can remarry after age sixty and claim benefit payments based on your former spouse's work. Beginning at age sixty-two, you could get benefits based on your new spouse's work if those benefits are higher. If you are divorced, your former wife or husband can claim survivor's payments at age sixty or older if the marriage lasted at least ten years.

Five Strategies to Boost Your Social Security Payments

Your Social Security monthly payments change based on your work history, marital status, and the age at which you elect to begin receiving benefits. Here are five ways you can significantly increase the amount you will receive from Social Security:

Earn More While Working

Negotiating for raises, working a second job, or anything else you do that boosts your annual earnings will also increase your Social Security payments in retirement. The government factors earned income of up to $118,500 per year into your Social Security payments.

Work for at Least Thirty-Five Years

The thirty-five years in which you earn the highest salary are used to calculate your Social Security payments. It's important to work for at least thirty-five years because zeros are averaged in for people who work fewer years. Working for more than thirty-five years can improve your payments if you are now earning more than you did earlier in your career.

Delay Claiming Your Payments

While you can sign up for Social Security payments at age sixty-two, payments are significantly reduced if you start them before your full retirement age. You can get the full Social Security payment you have earned at your full retirement age, which is typically age sixty-six or sixty-seven. Social Security payments will increase for each year you delay claiming your payments up until age seventy. After age seventy there is no additional benefit to waiting to sign up for Social Security.

Coordinate Benefits with Your Spouse

If you're married, you are eligible to claim spousal payments worth up to 50 percent of the higher earner's benefit if that's more than you can get based on your own work record. You need to claim spousal payments at your full retirement age to get half of the higher earner's benefit amount. Spousal payouts are reduced for early claiming.

Factor In Survivor's Benefits

Husbands and wives are eligible for survivor payments when their spouse passes away. If you are the higher-earning member of the couple, you can increase the amount your surviving spouse will receive by delaying when you sign up for your Social Security payments.

Claim Disability Benefits

Social Security payments are not just for retired people. If you become disabled to the point that you can no longer work, you may be eligible for Social Security disability payments.

To qualify for disability payments, your medical condition must significantly limit your ability to do basic work activities, including walking, sitting, and remembering, for at least one year. The condition must prevent you from being able to do the work you did before the disability began or a different job for which you are qualified. You will need to provide medical records and test results about your condition and why it will prevent you from working. There is a list of severe medical conditions that are considered disabling, but you could also make the case that another condition is as debilitating as the illnesses on the list.

It can take a long time to process an application for disability benefits. The typical beneficiary receives a response in three to five months. Social Security disability benefits start sixth months after your disability began. For example, if your disability started on January 15, your disability payment eligibility begins in July. However, you won't receive the payment until August, because Social Security benefits are paid the month after they are due. If you disagree with the decision made about your claim, you can appeal it.

Apply for Family Benefits

The children of people who are retired or disabled may also qualify for Social Security payments. A biological child, adopted child, or dependent stepchild is eligible for Social Security payments if he or she has a parent who qualifies for Social Security retirement or disability benefits or who passed away after paying into Social Security.

To qualify for payments a child must be under age eighteen and unmarried. Payments usually stop after age eighteen, but full-time high school students can continue to receive payments at age nineteen. Dependent children who become disabled prior to age twenty-two can also continue to receive payments after age eighteen.

A spouse who is caring for a dependent child may qualify for additional payments. These payments typically end when the child turns age sixteen. However, if your child is severely disabled to the point that you have decision-making responsibility or perform personal services for him or her, payments might continue after age sixteen.

There are limits on how much family members of retired and disabled Social Security beneficiaries can receive. A child can qualify for as much as 50 percent of the parent's retirement or disability benefit or 75 percent of a deceased parent's Social Security payment. But there's also a family maximum of 150–180 percent of the parent's full benefit amount. If the benefits payable to all family members exceed this limit, each person's benefit is reduced proportionately.

The family maximum tends to impact households with three or more beneficiaries claiming on the same work record. The Social Security Administration estimates that about 200,000 families of retired workers and an additional 200,000 survivors of deceased workers have their benefits reduced by the family maximum. The median benefit for families of retired workers is $2,886 before applying the family maximum and $2,482 afterward, a decrease of about 14 percent for each family member. Among survivor families, benefits decline from $3,584 before the maximum to $2,401 afterward.

The State of Social Security

The Social Security Board of Trustees releases an annual report about the Social Security system's finances. The most recent annual checkup found that the program expects to have resources to distribute scheduled benefits until 2034. After that, the Social Security system will have enough tax revenue to pay out 79 percent of scheduled benefits. There are a variety of ways to fix this funding shortfall, including a payroll tax increase, increasing or eliminating the Social Security tax cap for high earners, a benefit cut, changing how the cost-of-living adjustment is calculated, raising the age at which workers are eligible for Social Security benefits, or a combination of several of these fixes. It's important for you to follow the political discussion about how to resolve this issue.

Working in Retirement

While working before retirement almost always increases your Social Security benefit, working after you sign up for Social Security could temporarily reduce your payments. If you are younger than your full retirement age, as a Social Security beneficiary you can earn up to $15,720 in 2016 without affecting your payments. If you earn above that amount, $1 in benefit payments will be temporarily withheld for every $2 earned above the limit. The year you turn your full retirement age the earnings limit jumps to $41,880 in 2016, and the amount withheld decreases to $1 in benefits withheld for every $3 earned above the limit. There's also a one-year exception to the earnings limits for people who retire mid-year. These earnings limits are adjusted to keep up with inflation each year.

Once you turn your full retirement age you can earn any amount without impacting your Social Security payments. If you did have benefits withheld, your payment will be recalculated when you turn your full retirement age to give you credit for the withheld earnings. If your earnings in retirement were higher than any of the years used to compute your original benefit, your benefit payment will also be recalculated with the higher earnings factored in.

Taxes on Social Security Payments

If Social Security is your only source of retirement income, you probably won't have to pay tax on your Social Security payments in retirement. But if you have other forms of retirement income you might have to pay tax on part of your benefit. About 40 percent of Social Security beneficiaries pay taxes on a portion of their Social Security benefit payments.

If the sum of your adjusted gross income, nontaxable interest, and half of your Social Security benefit exceeds $25,000 for individuals and $32,000 for couples, income tax could be due on up to 50 percent of your Social Security benefit. If your retirement income tops $34,000 for individuals and $44,000 for couples, up to 85 percent of your Social Security payments may be taxable. These thresholds are not adjusted for inflation, so more people will be subject to Social Security taxes over time.

Collecting Your Benefit

You can sign up for Social Security payments online at *www.ssa.gov*, by phone at 1-800-772-1213, or at a local Social Security office. You may need to provide some documents during the application process. Before you apply for benefits you should locate your Social Security number, birth certificate, and a copy of your W-2 forms or self-employment tax return from the previous year. You could also be asked to provide military service papers if you served, and proof of citizenship if you were not born in the United States. You will need to know your bank account number and routing number to set up direct deposit of your benefits into your account.

You probably won't ever get a paper Social Security check. New Social Security beneficiaries have been required to sign up for electronic payments since 2011. Retirees can elect to receive their payments by direct deposit to a bank or credit union account or loaded onto a prepaid debit card. When payments are delivered depends on your date of birth. Retirees whose birthday falls between the first and tenth of the month get payments on the second Wednesday of the month; those born between the eleventh and twentieth will receive their direct deposit on the third Wednesday; and people born on the twenty-first of the month or later get their payments on the fourth Wednesday.

Take Your Social Security Payments on the Road

If you travel to or live in a foreign country, you can still receive Social Security payments, though not Medicare benefits. However, there are a few countries where Social Security payments can't be sent, including Azerbaijan, Belarus, Georgia, Kazakhstan, Kyrgyzstan, Moldova, Tajikistan, Turkmenistan, Ukraine, Uzbekistan, and Vietnam.

Social Security statements listing your annual earnings, taxes paid into Social Security, and an estimate of how much you will receive in retirement are mailed to workers every five years between ages twenty-five and sixty. However, you can view your statement at any time online by creating an online account at *www.ssa.gov/myaccount*. These statements give you a personalized estimate of how much you will receive if you sign up for Social Security at your full retirement age, at age sixty-two, and at age seventy. They will also explain the payments you will be eligible for if you become disabled and how much your family members might qualify for when you pass away. It's important to periodically check these statements, especially with your tax return handy, to make sure your earnings and the taxes you paid are being properly recorded so that you can get the full Social Security benefit for which you are eligible.

STEP TAKEAWAYS

- Social Security will be among your most important sources of income in retirement, so it's important to learn how to maximize it.

- Social Security is based on your average income from thirty-five years of work. If you did not work for a total of thirty-five years, the zeros for those years when you didn't work will lower your average and, therefore, your payment.

- If you don't wait until your full retirement age, typically age sixty-six or sixty-seven, before claiming your benefits you will permanently lower your monthly payments. You can increase your Social Security payments by delaying claiming them up until age seventy.

- Coordinate your Social Security payments with your spouse to maximize your retirement and survivor's benefits as a couple.

- You can qualify for Social Security payments if you become disabled.

- Your Social Security benefits can be taxed, but only if your retirement income exceeds certain levels.

STEP 2

MAKE THE MOST OF MEDICARE

Signing up for Medicare is a major retirement milestone: *www.ssa.gov/ medicare/apply.html*. Once you qualify for this government health insurance program at age sixty-five, you can no longer be charged higher health insurance premiums because of a pre-existing condition or lose your health coverage due to job loss. As long as you continue to pay the premiums, which are typically deducted from your Social Security check, you are guaranteed health insurance coverage that will last the rest of your life.

Where Did Medicare Come From?

The Medicare program was signed into law in 1965 by President Lyndon Johnson, and retirees were first able to sign up in 1966. Former President Harry Truman was the first Medicare beneficiary. Truman's share of the cost, $3 per month, was deducted from his Social Security checks to pay for the insurance. Today the program provides health coverage for more than 55 million Americans.

Almost all working Americans pay into the Medicare system. Most workers contribute 1.45 percent of their earnings to the Medicare trust fund, and companies pay a matching 1.45 percent for each employee. Self-employed workers pay 2.9 percent of their earned income into the trust fund. There's an additional 0.9 percent tax on earnings that exceed

$200,000 for individuals and $250,000 for couples. Medicare coverage can begin as early as the month you turn sixty-five.

While signing up for Medicare is a relief for many people, it also comes with a complicated set of rules and sometimes significant out-of-pocket costs. There are four basic components of Medicare:

1. Medicare Part A is hospital insurance that covers inpatient care at a hospital, hospice care, and some types of home health care.
2. Medicare Part B is medical insurance that covers doctor's visits, outpatient care, and some preventive services.
3. Medicare Part C or Medicare Advantage Plans are a private-sector alternative to original Medicare in which you receive your Medicare Parts A, B, and D and other services from Medicare-approved private insurance companies, typically with additional restrictions on coverage.
4. Medicare Part D was added to the program in 2003 and provides prescription drug coverage.

You can also purchase Medicare supplemental policies called Medigap to cover some of the out-of-pocket costs of original Medicare or additional services.

Just like private health insurance, Medicare has deductibles and coinsurance, and there's no limit on how high your out-of-pocket costs can climb. However, there are steps you can take to minimize the medical bills you will receive as a Medicare beneficiary. There are even a variety of Medicare services you are entitled to for free. In this step, you'll learn how to make the most of your Medicare benefit.

Sign Up on Time

You can sign up for Medicare Part A hospital insurance and Part B medical insurance beginning three months before the month you turn sixty-five.

- If you sign up during the three months leading up to your sixty-fifth birthday, coverage can begin as early as the first day of your birth month.
- If your birthday falls on the first of the month, your coverage can start on the first day of the prior month.
- If you wait until your birth month or the three months following your sixty-fifth birthday to sign up for Medicare, your coverage could be delayed.

If you're already receiving Social Security benefits, you will automatically get Medicare Part A and Part B starting the first day of the month you turn sixty-five. You should receive a Medicare card in the mail three months before your sixty-fifth birthday.

Medicare Eligibility Windows

There are eligibility windows to sign up for Medicare Parts B and D, Medicare Advantage Plans, and Medigap plans. If you fail to sign up during these initial enrollment periods you could face higher premiums throughout your retirement. You can first sign up for Medicare Parts B and D and Medicare Advantage Plans during the seven-month period that begins three months before the month you turn sixty-five. Medigap policies have a different initial enrollment period that begins on the first day of the month in which you're sixty-five or older *and* enrolled in Part B. If you fail to enroll in Medicare during these sign-up periods you could be charged higher premiums for the rest of your life once you do sign up.

If you don't enroll in Medicare during the seven-month initial enrollment period around your sixty-fifth birthday, you can sign up between January 1 and March 31 each year. In this case, the coverage will begin on July 1 of the same year. However, if you don't claim Medicare Part B when you are first eligible, you might have to pay permanently higher premiums due to late enrollment. Monthly Part B premiums increase by 10 percent for each twelve-month period you were eligible for Medicare Part B but delayed claiming it. For example, if the seven-month initial enrollment period around your sixty-fifth birthday ended on September 30, 2011, but you didn't sign up for Medicare Part B until March 2014, your premiums will be 20 percent higher for the rest of your life due to the two full years of delay.

FOR EXAMPLE

Abigail's initial enrollment period to sign up for Medicare Part B, the seven-month window around her sixty-fifth birthday, ended on August 31, 2012, but she never got around to filling out the forms. She didn't sign up for Medicare Part B until March 2015, during the general enrollment period from January 1 to March 31 each year. Medicare Part B premiums increase by 10 percent for each 12-month period she was eligible for Medicare Part B but didn't sign up for it. While Abigail delayed signing up for thirty months, only two full twelve-month periods passed, so her monthly Medicare Part B premiums increased by 20 percent. Instead of paying the standard Medicare Part B premium of $104.90 per month in 2015, she pays $125.88 monthly, a penalty of $251.76 per year more. This 20 percent penalty will be applied to her premiums for the rest of her life.

Abigail also signed up for Medicare Part D prescription drug coverage thirty months after her initial enrollment period ended. The Medicare Part D late enrollment penalty is calculated by multiplying 1 percent of the national base beneficiary premium, which is $33.13 in 2015, by the number of full months she went without prescription drug coverage and rounded to the nearest 10 cents. So, Abigail will have a penalty of $9.90 per month added to her Medicare Part D premiums in 2015, which would cost her $118.80 over the course of a full year.

The Medicare Part D late enrollment penalty also increases over time. The national base beneficiary premium that is used to calculate the penalty may increase each year, and when it does, the penalty amount also increases. When the national base beneficiary premium grows to $34.10 in 2016, Abigail's penalty increases to $10.20 per month, or $122.40 for the year. This amount is added to the premium for any Medicare Part D plan Abigail selects. The lesson Abigail learned: Sign up on time!

If you didn't sign up for Medicare around your sixty-fifth birthday because you or your spouse was still working and covered by a group health insurance plan through your job, you can avoid the late enrollment penalty if you sign up within eight months of leaving the job or the coverage ending. Retiree health insurance and COBRA coverage do not count as health coverage based on current employment for the purposes of avoiding the late enrollment penalty.

You can sign up for Medicare online at *www.socialsecurity.gov/medicare/apply.html, www.ssa.gov,* in person at a Social Security office, or by calling 1-800-772-1213.

Plan for Costs

Medicare beneficiaries need to pay a variety of out-of-pocket costs. Premiums are the most predictable costs you will face. If you have already signed up for Social Security payments, your Medicare premiums will be automatically withheld from your benefit. If you haven't yet signed up for Social Security when you sign up for Medicare Part B, you will get a bill. Most people don't pay a monthly premium for Part A coverage if they paid Medicare taxes while working.

Most Medicare Part B beneficiaries (about 70 percent) will pay a $104.90 per month premium in 2016. Medicare Part B premiums are prevented by law from increasing faster than Social Security payments for most existing beneficiaries. There was no Social Security cost-of-living adjustment in 2016, so Social Security beneficiaries pay the same premium they paid in 2015. However, people who haven't yet signed up for Social Security or first enroll in Medicare Part B in 2016 will pay a slightly higher Medicare Part B premium of $121.80 per month, because they are not protected from premium increases. Those with modified adjusted gross incomes above $85,000 for individuals and $170,000 for couples also pay higher Part B premiums.

Like private health insurance, Medicare also has many cost-sharing requirements. The Medicare Part B deductible is $166 in 2016, after which you must pay 20 percent of the Medicare-approved amount for each service. There is no annual limit on how much you might need to pay out of pocket. If you are hospitalized, Medicare Part A carries a $1,288 deductible. If you spend more than sixty days in the hospital you will be charged $322 each day for days 61 through 90, and $644 per day for up to 60 lifetime reserve days after that. If you use up all your lifetime reserve days you will become responsible for all hospitalization costs after that. The costs for Medicare Parts C and D vary depending on the plan you select.

Make the Most of Your Benefit

Medicare covers many preventive services that older people need to detect potential health problems with no cost-sharing requirements. During your first twelve months as a Medicare Part B beneficiary you are eligible for a free "Welcome to Medicare" preventive care doctor's visit. After that, you are eligible for a free wellness visit once every twelve months. Medicare also covers a variety of preventive care services without any extra out-of-pocket costs. These include cardiovascular disease screenings, mammograms, flu shots, and bone mass measurements.

However, if a problem is discovered during a free preventive care visit or screening and additional tests or procedures are performed, additional costs could apply. For example, colonoscopies are typically covered once every 120 months with no out-of-pocket costs. But if a doctor finds a polyp and removes it during the colonoscopy, then you could get a bill. You may have to pay 20 percent of the Medicare-approved amount for the doctor's services and a copayment to the medical facility where the procedure was performed.

Add a Supplemental Plan

Medicare recipients can face significant medical-care costs if they develop a serious or chronic condition, including deductibles, copays, and 20 percent coinsurance for many covered services. There is no limit to how high these cost-sharing requirements might climb. The best way to protect yourself from these potentially high health-care costs is to supplement Medicare with another insurance plan that will cover some of these out-of-pocket expenses.

Medigap Plans

Medigap policies are additional insurance sold by private insurance companies, which can be used to pay for the copayments, coinsurance, and deductibles of traditional Medicare. Some Medigap plans might also pay for additional services that traditional Medicare doesn't cover. Medigap policies can help to make your retirement health-care costs more predictable. Instead of the potentially unlimited out-of-pocket costs you could face due to the copays and coinsurance for each covered service with Medicare Parts A and B, you pay a monthly premium to an insurance company, which takes on the risk of your out-of-pocket costs.

It's important to purchase a Medigap policy during the six-month period that begins on the first day of the month in which you are sixty-five or older and enrolled in Medicare Part B. After this initial enrollment period a Medigap policy can cost significantly more or you may be denied the right to purchase one. Medigap insurance companies are allowed to use medical underwriting to decide whether to accept a patient and how much to charge for the policy. However, during this one-time open enrollment period you can buy any Medigap policy the company sells, regardless of any health conditions you have, for the same price as someone in good health. If you delay signing up for Medicare Part B past age sixty-five due to coverage from your current employer, the Medigap open enrollment period starts when you sign up for Part B. After your Medigap open enrollment period ends there's no guarantee that an insurance company will sell you a Medigap policy if you have any health problems.

Medigap policies are standardized and must provide certain basic benefits. Many plans will cover your Medicare Part B coinsurance and copayments and pay for hospital costs for an additional 365 days after Medicare benefits are used up. Some plans will also cover your deductibles for Medicare Parts A and B. If you plan to travel overseas in retirement, you can select a policy that includes foreign travel emergency health-care coverage at medical facilities outside the United States. The premiums for Medigap policies can vary widely, even for the same coverage, so it's important to shop around for the plan that meets your needs for the most affordable price. Medigap policies are guaranteed to be renewable, even if you have health problems. The private insurance company can't cancel your Medigap policy as long as you pay the premium.

Medicare Advantage Plans

When you sign up for a Medicare Advantage Plan, which is sometimes called Medicare Part C, you get your Medicare Parts A and B through this private plan instead of original Medicare. Medicare Advantage Plans are required to cover most of the services that original Medicare covers. They sometimes offer extra coverage, such as vision, dental, or wellness programs, often in exchange for an additional premium. However, Medicare Advantage Plans have different out-of-pocket costs for covered services and sometimes more coverage restrictions than traditional Medicare, and these rules can change each year. Medicare Advantage Plans are sometimes health maintenance organizations (HMOs) that will only cover services at doctors or hospitals in the plan's network and require referrals from your primary care doctor for tests or to see specialists. They could also be preferred provider organizations (PPOs), which allow you to pay less out of pocket when you see preferred health-care providers but charge more if you select other health-care facilities. The Medicare Advantage program also includes private fee-for-service plans in which the plan determines how much you will need to pay out of pocket each time you receive care and special needs plans that cater to specific groups of people with specialized health-care requirements.

In some Medicare Advantage Plans you need to use plan doctors, hospitals, and other approved providers or you may be responsible for paying more or all of the costs of the services you receive.

Sign Up for Prescription Drug Coverage

If you're enrolled in Medicare Part D, you have a lot of choices to make regarding your prescription drug coverage. Seniors have to choose among an average of twenty-six different plans. If you want to get the best possible coverage and the best value for your money, you will need to shop around for a new plan each year throughout your retirement.

You become eligible for Medicare Part D during a seven-month window that begins three months before your sixty-fifth birthday. It's important to sign up during this initial enrollment period because there is a late enrollment penalty that is added to your Part D premium if you go sixty-three or more days without prescription drug coverage.

The penalty increases the longer you go without prescription drug coverage. It is calculated by multiplying 1 percent of the "national base beneficiary premium," ($34.10 in 2016) by the number of months you went without prescription drug coverage since qualifying for Medicare. That amount is rounded to the nearest ten cents and added to your premiums for the rest of your life.

The average premium for a Medicare Part D prescription drug plan was $32 in 2015, but costs can vary considerably by region and the coverage option you select. Premiums are higher for individuals with incomes above $85,000 and couples earning more than $170,000. Part D plans are also allowed to charge deductibles of up to $360 in 2016, although some Part D plans charge a lower deductible, often in exchange for higher premiums.

Other Out-of-Pocket Costs

Once you meet the deductible, there are other types of out-of-pocket costs you may face. Each Part D plan has a formulary or list of covered medications, which are often sorted into tiers with different prices. Drugs on each tier may have a set copayment for each medication, such as $15, or require you to pay coinsurance, which is a percentage of the cost of the drug. Part D plans are allowed to change their formularies each year, so you will need to check to be sure that ongoing medications or prescriptions you might need will continue to be covered at an affordable price in the coming year.

Here are some other possible issues:

- Medications can be removed from the plan's formulary. A drug that was covered last year might not be covered at all the following year or could be moved to a different formulary tier with bigger cost-sharing requirements.
- A plan might require prior authorization before you can fill certain prescriptions or mandate that you try a similar lower-cost drug before the plan will cover a more expensive medication.
- There may be rules about where and how you can fill your prescriptions. Some prescription drug plans have preferred pharmacy networks, and charge participants higher prices if they don't fill their prescriptions at the desired pharmacies.
- There may be quantity limits on how much medication you can get at a time.

Given all of this, you may find it to be worth paying slightly higher premiums to be able to use a pharmacy that is close to home or avoid cumbersome medication restrictions.

Most Medicare Part D plans have a coverage gap, often referred to as the donut hole. The coverage gap begins when you've spent $3,310 on covered drugs in 2016. While in the gap you will be responsible for 45 percent of the cost for your covered brand-name prescription drugs and 58 percent of the price of generic medications. Some Part D plans offer additional gap coverage in exchange for higher premiums. Once you've spent $4,850 out of pocket in 2016, catastrophic coverage kicks in and you will only need to pay a copayment and coinsurance for your medications for the rest of the year.

Medicare Plan Finder

You can use the Medicare Plan Finder (*www.medicare.gov/find-a-plan*) to examine how all the available Part D plans in your area will cover the drugs you need. This online tool gives you a chart that explains the premiums, deductibles, copays, coinsurance, and drug restrictions for each plan.

Medicare recipients are given the opportunity to switch Medicare Part D plans once a year during the open enrollment period from October 15 to December 7. Even if you are happy with your current coverage, it's a good idea to get into the habit of shopping around for a new plan each year because your medical needs and the medications covered by your plan are likely to change. Take a moment to consider which medications you currently use or might use in the coming year and evaluate which plan will cover you best going forward. Plans change their formularies and how much beneficiaries are charged for drugs each year. Even if your medications were covered in the past, that does not mean they will continue to be covered in the same way or at all in the future. It's important to examine all the costs of your medications, including the deductible, copayments, and coinsurance, and not simply focus on the monthly plan premium.

High Income, Higher Premiums

As of 2016, most retirees pay the standard Medicare Part B premium of $104.90 and new enrollees in 2016 pay $121.80. However, retirees with high incomes pay more. Those individuals earning $85,000–$107,000 ($170,000–$214,000 for couples) pay $170.50 per month. Premiums climb to $243.60 monthly for individuals earning $107,000–$160,000 ($214,000–$320,000 for couples). Retirees bringing in $160,000–

$214,000 ($320,000–$428,000 for couples) pay $316.70 per month for Medicare Part B. And if your income tops $214,000 ($428,000 for couples) your Medicare Part B premium will be $389.80.

FOR EXAMPLE

Sophia needs to take three medicines each day. She wants to purchase a prescription drug plan that covers her medications at the best possible price. She would prefer to use a pharmacy close to her home in Asheville, North Carolina. She goes to the Medicare Plan Finder website, types in her medications, and discovers that she has twenty-six plan options in her area that cover all of her medications.

The monthly premiums on these plans range from $15.20 to $133.50. But the situation is not as simple as picking the plan with the lowest premium. Some of the plans have deductibles as high as $360 before any medication expenses will be covered, while others have no deductible. Sophia needs to factor this into the annual plan cost. If she chooses the plan with the $15.20 monthly premium, she will pay $182.40 in annual premium costs, plus a $360 deductible before her medications will be covered, for a total annual cost of $542.40.

Some plans also require beneficiaries to pay a set dollar amount or percentage of the price each time they fill a prescription. The copays range from $1 to $85, and in some cases the coinsurance could be as high as 50 percent of the cost of the medicine. The plan with the $15.20 monthly premium also has copays between $1 and $4 per prescription and coinsurance that ranges from 20 percent to 35 percent of the cost of each drug. The plan with the $23.10 monthly premium, but no annual deductible, has copays that range from $7 to $37, depending on the drug, and coinsurance that could be as high as 47 percent of the cost of the medication.

Sophia should review all these options when considering which plan to choose and find the plan that makes financial sense—not just in terms of its premiums, but with regard to deductibles, prescription costs, and ease of use.

Medicare Part D beneficiaries with high incomes also pay more. In addition to the premium for the plan they select, an additional premium is added to their bill. For people with incomes between $85,000 and $107,000 ($170,000 to $214,000 for couples), $12.70 is added to the monthly premium. The premium grows to $32.80 per month for retirees earning between $107,000 and $160,000 ($214,000 to $320,000 for couples) in annual income. The Medicare Part D premium increases to $52.80 for individuals with incomes of $160,000 to $214,000 ($320,000 to $428,000 for couples). And if your retirement income exceeds $214,000 ($428,000 for couples), your Medicare Part D premium jumps $72.90 per month.

What Medicare Doesn't Cover

Older people need a variety of common medical services that Medicare doesn't cover or only covers under specific circumstances. Don't expect Medicare to pay for these health-care costs:

Eyeglasses and Eye Care

Many older Americans need glasses or contact lenses to see clearly, but Medicare typically won't pay for them. Most Medicare beneficiaries will get a vision check at their annual preventive care visit, and some diagnostic tests for eye conditions such as glaucoma are covered, but Medicare doesn't cover routine eye exams or fittings for eyeglasses or contact lenses. Eyeglasses are covered only for people who have received cataract surgery that implants an intraocular lens.

Dental Care

Medicare won't pay for routine dental care, such as checkups, cleanings, and fillings. Dentures and the fittings for them also aren't covered. Certain dental services that are performed while a person is hospitalized during an emergency may be covered.

Hearing Aids and Exams

Medicare Part B covers hearing and balance exams that are ordered by a doctor, but it won't cover routine hearing exams. Hearing aids and the exams for fitting an appropriate device are not covered by Medicare.

Cosmetic Surgery

Medicare will only cover cosmetic surgery if the procedure is performed because of an injury or illness. For example, a breast prosthesis is covered if you have had a mastectomy as part of treatment for breast cancer.

Acupuncture

Medicare won't pay for this traditional Chinese medicine procedure, which involves inserting needles into the skin at specific parts of the body.

Overseas Services

Medicare typically won't pay for health-care bills incurred while living or traveling outside the United States. However, Medicare will cover medical services received while onboard a ship in U.S. territorial waters or treatments received in the U.S. territories of Puerto Rico, the U.S. Virgin Islands, Guam, the Northern Mariana Islands, and American Samoa. Services will also be covered during an emergency if you are treated at a Canadian hospital while traveling between Alaska and the continental United States or if a foreign hospital is closer than the nearest U.S. hospital when an injury occurs in the United States.

Long-Term Care

Medicare beneficiaries are limited to 100 days of covered long-term care, after which they become responsible for all costs. Those with low incomes and assets may be able to qualify for Medicaid, which will pay for some forms of long-term care such as nursing homes. Retirees with assets to protect may want to purchase a long-term care insurance policy to help pay for potential nursing home costs.

Nursing Home Care

Medicare will cover short-term stays at a nursing facility for a limited amount of time following a hospital stay of at least three days. You won't have any out-of-pocket costs for the first twenty days of care, but for days twenty-one through 100 your out-of-pocket cost jumps to $157.50 per day. Medicare won't pay for nursing home stays that exceed 100 days.

STEP TAKEAWAYS

- To avoid permanently higher premiums, sign up for Medicare Parts B and D and Medigap on time when you turn sixty-five or leave a job with group health insurance.

- Take advantage of Medicare's free annual wellness and preventive care services, but watch out for additional costs if a problem is discovered and additional tests or procedures are ordered.

- Budget for the common medical services older people need that Medicare doesn't cover, including eyeglasses, dentures, hearing aids, and long-term care.

- Purchase a Medigap plan to cover some of the out-of-pocket costs that traditional Medicare doesn't cover.

- Shop around for a new Medicare Part D plan each year during the open enrollment period, and double-check that your medications will continue to be covered with reasonable out-of-pocket costs.

STEP 3

BOOST YOUR 401(K) BALANCE

401(k) plans are now the predominant form of workplace retirement benefit. These savings accounts allow you to defer paying income tax on the amount you contribute until you withdraw the money from the account. Unlike those who have traditional pension plans, individual employees who have a 401(k) plan must take on the responsibility of making appropriate saving and investing decisions. It is up to you to decide how much to contribute, how to invest your savings, and how to protect your nest egg from losses.

401(k) plans are often referred to as defined contribution plans, because you and your employer are each free to decide how much to contribute to the plan and can elect to change that amount at any time. The benefit you will get from a 401(k) plan in retirement is not guaranteed, and 401(k) accounts can lose value when the investments you select decline. Traditional pension plans are called defined benefit plans because the retirement payout to workers is guaranteed once they meet certain job tenure and age requirements, and the responsibility to fund them rests with the employer.

401(k) plans get their odd name from the Internal Revenue Code that created these accounts in 1978. Some companies give their retirement accounts a more descriptive name, but 401(k) has become a household word. Companies flocked to 401(k) plans because they are a less costly form of retirement benefit for employers to fund, and the employer doesn't have ongoing responsibilities to provide income to former employees. 401(k) plans are also more portable than pension plans; frequent job-changers who would have missed out on a pension plan can take their 401(k) savings with them. However, employees who don't save consistently are likely to get less retirement income from a 401(k) plan than they would have gotten under a traditional pension system.

There are a variety of ways to painlessly increase your 401(k) balance, including getting an employer match and having your contributions automatically withheld from your paychecks. But equally important is protecting your 401(k) balance from decline due to taxes, excessive fees, and early withdrawal penalties. In addition to saving consistently, you also have to make smart investment decisions that will help your money grow and protect your savings from losses. A 401(k), used correctly, packs the triple punch of automated saving, tax breaks, and employer contributions. Try the following strategies to maximize the value of your 401(k) plan.

Maximize Your Tax Break

You can defer paying income tax on up to $18,000 in 2016 by contributing that amount to a 401(k) plan. Those age fifty and older are eligible to make catch-up contributions worth an extra $6,000. So, older workers can claim a tax deduction on as much as $24,000 in contributions to a 401(k) plan in 2016. These contribution limits are adjusted each year to keep up with inflation.

To max out your 401(k), you will need to contribute $1,500 per month or $750 per bimonthly paycheck. Older workers need to save $2,000 per month or $1,000 per twice monthly paycheck to get the maximum possible tax savings from their 401(k) plan. Contributions to 401(k) plans are typically due by the end of the calendar year.

The tax savings you get by contributing to a traditional 401(k) plan can be enormous. If you're in the 25 percent tax bracket and contribute $5,000 to a 401(k), you will save $1,250 on your current tax bill. If you're in your fifties, are in the 25 percent tax bracket, and completely max out your 401(k) by contributing $24,000, you will reduce your income tax bill by $6,000. Since 401(k) contributions are withheld directly from your pay, the tax savings is realized immediately in each paycheck. Due to the tax deferral, a $100 401(k) contribution will only reduce your take-home pay by $75 if you are in the 25 percent tax bracket. Income tax won't be due on your 401(k) contributions until you withdraw the money from the account.

Those in high tax brackets typically have the most to gain by contributing to 401(k) plans, but there are also savings perks for people earning smaller salaries. Those with incomes below $30,750 for individuals, $46,125 for heads of household, and $61,500 for couples in 2016 who save for retirement in a 401(k) are eligible for the saver's credit. This valuable tax credit can be worth as much as $1,000 for individuals and $2,000 for couples, although most people get between $100 and $200. The saver's credit can be claimed in addition to the tax deduction for traditional 401(k) contributions. Full-time students, those under age eighteen, and people who are claimed as a dependent on someone else's tax return are not eligible for the saver's credit.

You can claim the saver's credit on 401(k) contributions of up to $2,000 for individuals and $4,000 for couples. The credit ranges from 10 percent to 50 percent of the amount contributed, with the biggest credits going to people with the lowest incomes. For example, a couple earning $30,000 who puts $1,000 in a 401(k) could earn a 50 percent credit worth $500, in addition to the tax deduction on their $1,000 contribution. A couple earning $58,000 who contributes the same amount to a 401(k) would get a 10 percent credit worth $100.

Sign Up As Soon As You Can

Some employers allow you to begin saving in the 401(k) plan with your first paycheck, while others impose a waiting period of up to a year before new employees are allowed to participate in the plan. If you can't sign up right away, make a note of the date your 401(k) eligibility begins and take care to enroll when the waiting period ends.

Set Up Automatic Contributions

Contributing to a 401(k) via payroll deduction is one of the most convenient ways to save for retirement. The money never hits your checking account, so it's not easy to spend it. Furthermore, the money will continue to accumulate and grow in your account without you having to do much else. Some plans also have an escalation feature that over time will automatically increase the percentage of your paychecks you save. If your plan doesn't have that feature or you don't agree with the rate at which it automatically increases your savings rate, you should consider boosting the percentage of your salary you save as you get raises and bonuses.

Don't Stick with the Defaults

New employees and sometimes existing workers are increasingly likely to be automatically enrolled in a 401(k) plan. This means that your employer withholds a portion of your paycheck and deposits it in a 401(k) plan on your behalf unless you take action to opt out. The most common default savings rate is 3 percent of pay. But sticking with that default savings rate—while certainly better than saving nothing at all—isn't likely to produce enough income to maintain your lifestyle in retirement. Automatic enrollment typically gets more people to enroll in the plan than would voluntarily enroll, but employees who are automatically enrolled in 401(k) plans tend to save at a lower rate than workers who choose to sign up with the plan. To try to correct this problem, some 401(k) plans have automatic escalation, which gradually increases your savings rate over time until you reach a target savings rate determined by the plan sponsor. Rather than passively accepting the defaults selected by your employer, take care to increase your savings rate to a level that is more likely to meet your retirement income needs.

Get an Employer Match

The fastest way to grow your 401(k) account balance is to get company contributions from your employer. Some employers contribute to a 401(k) plan on behalf of employees without workers having to save anything on their own. Nonmatching contributions are sometimes discretionary; the company may calculate the match as a percentage of the employee's pay or base it on company profits. Matching contributions are provided only to workers who save in the 401(k) plan. If your employer offers a matching contribution, it's important to find out what you need to do to take advantage of it.

The most common 401(k) match is 50 cents for each dollar saved up to 6 percent of pay. Clearly in this case you should save at least 6 percent of your salary in the 401(k) plan to get the maximum possible match. If you're earning $50,000 per year, you would need to contribute $3,000 to the 401(k) plan to get the entire match of $1,500. By contributing 6 percent of your salary, you get a match of 3 percent from your employer and in effect are saving a total of 9 percent of your salary in the 401(k) plan. However, if you chose to save only 3 percent of pay in the 401(k) plan or were automatically enrolled at that savings rate, you'll only get a 401(k) match of $750.

It can be difficult for short-term employees to get a 401(k) match. Some 401(k) plans require new employees to wait as long as a year before they are eligible for the match. Even once you qualify for a 401(k) match, you don't get to keep it when you leave the company unless you are vested in the 401(k) plan. Less than half of 401(k) plans immediately vest company contributions to the plan. Some companies don't let you keep any of the match when you leave the job unless you stayed with the company for a specific number of years, typically two or three. Other companies permit employees to keep a percentage of the company contributions to the 401(k) plan based on their years of service, but you typically don't get to keep all of it unless you stay with the company for at least five or six years. If you are close to becoming vested in your 401(k) plan, sticking around for the required amount of time could get you thousands of extra dollars for retirement.

When evaluating a job offer from a company it's important to consider the entire compensation package, including company 401(k) contributions. If two jobs both offer you the same salary, but one provides employer 401(k) contributions and the other doesn't, the job with the 401(k) match is offering you more overall compensation. But you should also consider how long you are planning to stay at the company and whether you will vest in the 401(k) plan and get to keep the match.

How to Get a 401(k) Match

A 401(k) match is likely to be the best return on your money you will ever get. If your employer gives you 50 cents for each dollar you contribute to a 401(k) plan, that's a 50 percent return before you even take into account any investment gains. If you work at a company that provides a dollar-for-dollar match, you are doubling your money.

To get a 401(k) match you need to meet certain requirements determined by your employer. But each 401(k) plan works slightly differently. Here are several important pieces of information you should find out about your 401(k) match:

How Much Is the Match?

Find out the percentage of your salary your employer is willing to contribute to your 401(k). Companies are not required to offer a 401(k) match, and can stop their 401(k) matching contributions at any time, so it's important to take advantage of a 401(k) match when it is offered. The most common 401(k) match is worth 3 percent of pay.

FOR EXAMPLE

John, Paul, and George are job-hoppers who want to build a nest egg for retirement. They each save $5,000 per year in the 401(k) plan at their respective jobs and get a 401(k) match worth 50 cents for each dollar they save. After two years on the job they each have $15,000 in a 401(k) account, including $10,000 they contributed and $5,000 in employer-matching contributions. They also each have another job offer that is too good to pass up.

How much of the $15,000 each employee gets to keep depends on the company vesting schedule. While all three workers can walk away with the $10,000 they personally contributed to the 401(k) plan and any investment gains it generated, only employees who are vested in the 401(k) plan get to keep employer contributions.

John, the most fortunate of the three, participated in a 401(k) plan with immediate vesting. He gets to keep the entire $15,000 401(k) plan balance, and can continue to defer taxes on it by leaving it in the 401(k) plan, rolling it over to an IRA, or transferring it to the 401(k) plan at his new company.

Paul's employer has a three-year cliff vesting schedule, which means employees don't get to keep any employer contributions to the 401(k) until they stay with the company for three years, after which they get to keep the entire amount contributed. Paul walks away from the job he held for two years with $10,000 and can't take any of his employer's contributions with him. The new job has a higher salary than his old one, but he needs to factor in leaving $5,000 in potential retirement income on the table.

George's 401(k) plan has a five-year graded vesting schedule, in which he gets to keep 20 percent of the company 401(k) contributions for each year of service until he hits five years of job tenure and is fully vested. Due to his two years of service, George gets to keep 40 percent of the $5,000 his employer contributed to the 401(k) plan, or $2,000, so he leaves his job with $12,000 in retirement savings.

What Do You Need to Do to Get the Match?

Some employers will contribute to a 401(k) plan on your behalf without your having to save anything. Others require employees to contribute before providing any company contributions. Find out how much you need to contribute to the 401(k) plan to get the maximum possible employer contribution. The most common saving requirement to get the maximum possible 401(k) match is 6 percent of pay.

When Do You Become Vested in the 401(k) Plan?

You don't get to keep employer contributions to your 401(k) until you are vested in the plan. Find out how long you need to stay at your current job before you can take the 401(k) match with you when you leave.

Carefully Select Your Investments

Most 401(k) plans have a limited menu of investment options to pick from. However, you don't need to invest in all of them to be diversified. One simple and low-cost way to invest is to split your contributions among a U.S. total stock market index fund, a U.S. total bond market index fund, and, if you want international exposure, an international total stock market index fund. These three funds will allow you to capture the overall returns of the major investment classes. When choosing among the funds in your 401(k) plan, also pay close attention to the fees charged by each investment option, which will be subtracted from your returns.

Broadly speaking, there are two types of mutual funds:

1. Actively managed mutual funds have a professional fund manager who decides what investments to buy and sell within the fund. When you invest in an actively managed fund you are counting on the skill of the fund manager to increase the fund

in value. Actively managed funds usually have high costs due to the compensation of the fund manager and the more active trading going on within the fund.

2. Passively managed index funds are diverse baskets of stocks that help you capture the returns of the entire stock market or a specific sector of the market. Index funds typically have much lower fees and thus tend to produce higher returns for investors.

If you are automatically enrolled in a 401(k) plan, your money will be invested in the plan's default investment. The most common default investment is a target-date fund. These allocate your retirement savings into a range of investments including equities, bonds, and cash and gradually shift the investment mix to become more conservative over time. However, it's important to closely examine your company's default investment to make sure it suits your investment needs and risk tolerance. Before you choose to stick with the default target-date fund, make sure that the underlying investments, rate at which the fund gets more conservative, fees, and target retirement date match your investment needs. If you are not comfortable with the target-date fund, you can select other investments offered by your 401(k) plan.

401(k) account owners typically choose a mix of stocks and bonds that suit their risk tolerance when they first sign up for the account. However, investment gains and losses will shift that balance, and you will need to periodically move money back to your target asset allocation. Rebalancing your portfolio helps you to avoid unintentionally taking on too much risk if the stock portion of your portfolio grows significantly faster than your bond and cash allocations. It also allows you to sell high, which locks in your stock market gains, and buy low, and then watch your investments grow during the subsequent recovery.

Minimize 401(k) Fees

The fees you pay on your retirement savings directly reduce your retirement account balance. You can't control your investment returns, but you do have a measure of control over the expense ratio of the funds you choose to invest in. Your 401(k) plan is required to send you a fee disclosure statement each year that gives you specific information about each investment option in your plan, including past investment performance and how that performance compares to a benchmark investment. For example, you can view how the performance of an S&P 500 index fund in your 401(k) plan compares to the actual returns of the S&P 500.

The 401(k) information will also list the annual gross expense ratio of each investment option, expressed as both a percentage of the account balance and the dollar cost for each $1,000 invested. This allows you to calculate how expensive the fund will be to own. For example, if you invest $5,000 in a fund that has an expense ratio of 0.52 percent, or $5.20 per $1,000 invested, you can easily determine that the fund will cost you $26 per year. You will owe this cost no matter how the investment performs. These fees are usually deducted from your investment return or account balance and may not be listed on each account statement you receive.

You can use your fee disclosure forms to compare the costs of all the funds in your 401(k) plan in each investment class. Index funds often have the lowest fees because they are simply tracking the entire market or a specific group of investments. Actively managed funds, on the other hand, tend to have higher costs because you are paying a fund manager to select investments for you within the fund. You should also look up shareholder fees or other restrictions that might cause you to incur fees on your investments.

In addition to the fees on each investment option, 401(k) plans also have a variety of administrative fees, perhaps including recordkeeping, accounting, and legal fees. These fees might be deducted from your account.

FOR EXAMPLE

Beth is saving $10,000 per year for retirement, but is frustrated that her account balance isn't growing fast enough to retire comfortably by the time she turns sixty-five. While she can't control her investment returns, she can make a few adjustments to promote growth.

The first of these has to do with tax breaks. Beth began her retirement planning with a savings account. Her $10,000 in savings earned 1 percent interest, or $100, on which she had to pay income tax. Since she is in the 25 percent tax bracket, she paid $25 in federal income tax on her $100 gain. The next year she instead elected to have $10,000 withheld from her paychecks on a pre-tax basis and deposited in a 401(k) account. This reduced her taxable income by $10,000, saving her $2,500 in withheld taxes. The investment gains generated in the account weren't taxed either. Beth won't have to pay income tax on this savings until she withdraws the money from the account.

A second way Beth can grow her retirement savings faster is by taking advantage of her employer's contributions to her 401(k). Beth's current employer contributes 50 cents for each dollar she saves in the 401(k) plan, which turns her $10,000 401(k) contributions into $15,000, which is a 50 percent return on her investment. However, she also has a job offer from another company that is willing to match her retirement account contributions dollar for dollar. This would turn her $10,000 401(k) contribution into $20,000, which effectively doubles her retirement savings.

Finally, Beth needs to reduce the fees she pays on her investments. She was invested in a blended fund comprised of a mix of stocks and bonds that had an annual expense ratio of 0.79 percent, which meant that this fund was costing her $79 for every $10,000 she invested in it. She decided that she could meet her investment goals with lower-cost funds. She moved 60 percent of her savings into an S&P 500 index fund with an expense ratio of 0.05 percent, and 40 percent into a bond index fund that costs 0.17 percent. This reduced her annual investment expense ratio to $9.80 for every $10,000 invested, a savings of $69.20.

Important Ages for a 401(k) Plan

Your age determines how much you can contribute to a 401(k) plan and when you should start withdrawing money from the account. Pay attention to these key ages when making decisions about your 401(k):

- Age **fifty.** Workers age fifty and older become eligible to make catch-up contributions to 401(k) plans, which means they can defer paying income tax on $6,000 more than younger people. The 401(k) contribution limit jumps from $18,000 at age forty-nine and younger to $24,000 at age fifty and older.
- Age **fifty-five.** If you leave your job in the year you turn fifty-five or later, you can take 401(k) withdrawals from the retirement account associated with the job you most recently left without having to pay the 10 percent early withdrawal penalty.
- Age **fifty-nine-and-a-half.** There is no longer a 10 percent early withdrawal penalty on 401(k) distributions taken after reaching this age.
- Age **seventy-and-a-half.** 401(k) distributions become required at this age, unless you are still working and don't have an ownership stake in the company. The penalty for missing a required minimum distribution is 50 percent of the amount that should have been withdrawn.

Avoid Early Withdrawals

It's prudent to maintain an emergency fund outside of your retirement accounts to cover unexpected bills. If an emergency expense should arise that you are unprepared for, there are a variety of ways to access your 401(k) money early, but each has drawbacks and fees.

As mentioned in the previous section, withdrawals from your 401(k) before age fifty-nine-and-a-half typically trigger a 10 percent early withdrawal penalty. However, retirees who leave their jobs in the year they turn age fifty-five or older (or age fifty for public safety employees) can take penalty-free 401(k) withdrawals from the 401(k) associated with their most recent job, although not from a previous 401(k) or IRA.

If you absolutely need to tap your retirement account early for an emergency expense, you can take a loan from it. 401(k) loans are typically less damaging to your retirement security than an early withdrawal because you pay yourself back with interest and there are no tax consequences. 401(k) participants are eligible to borrow up to 50 percent of their vested account balance up to $50,000 if their plan allows loans. For example, if your account balance is $30,000, you will be able to borrow up to $15,000. You need an account balance of at least $100,000 in order to be able to borrow the full $50,000. You must repay the loan in at least quarterly payments over five years, but the repayment period can be extended if you use the loan to purchase a home.

401(k) loans have a variety of costs and risks. These loans often charge origination, administration, and maintenance fees. Loans that are not paid back within five years are considered distributions from the 401(k) plan, which can trigger income tax and the early withdrawal penalty. And if you lose or leave your job, the loan becomes due. If you can't pay it back, the outstanding balance becomes subject to tax and potentially the early withdrawal penalty. Plus, you miss out on the market gains you could have gotten if you left your money in the account.

Some 401(k) plans allow early withdrawals for existing employees who can demonstrate an "immediate and heavy financial need" for the money. The IRS says circumstances that may qualify include medical expenses, the purchase or repair of a principal residence, education expenses, preventing eviction or foreclosure, and burial or funeral expenses.

However, hardship withdrawals often have a negative impact on your retirement savings. They trigger a 10 percent early withdrawal penalty for people under age fifty-nine-and-a-half and 20 percent withholding for income taxes. Also, workers who take hardship distributions are prohibited from making new contributions to the 401(k) plan for at least six months, so they miss out on getting an employer match and being able to defer income tax on their retirement savings.

Changing Jobs

Each time you change jobs you need to decide what to do with your former 401(k) plan. It can be tempting to cash out the balance when you leave a job, but early distributions from a 401(k) trigger significant taxes and penalties. If you withdraw $5,000 from your 401(k) when you leave a job you must pay income tax on that amount. And if you are under age fifty-five when you leave your job, you will also be charged a 10 percent early withdrawal penalty. For example, a fifty-year-old worker who is in the 25 percent tax bracket and withdraws $5,000 from his 401(k) will only get $3,250 after paying taxes and penalties on that withdrawal.

If you want to preserve the tax-deferred status of your 401(k) plan, you can leave the money in your old 401(k) plan if the balance exceeds $5,000, roll it over into your new employer's 401(k) if the plan allows it, or transfer the balance to an IRA. When deciding which option is best it helps to look at the investment options and fees that need to be paid to use each type of account. Some large 401(k) plans use their bargaining power to negotiate especially low fees and favorable investment options on behalf of participants, which could be a reason to stick with a 401(k) plan. Other 401(k) plans have unnecessarily high costs and poor investment selections, and a job change offers an opportunity to move your money to a better account.

If you have a 401(k) balance of only $1,000 to $5,000 when you leave your job and don't specify what should be done with the money, it could be automatically transferred to an IRA. A Government

Accountability Office report found that forced-transfer IRA accounts tend to have high fees and low investment returns. The account balances often decline over time, sometimes even to zero. If you have less than $1,000 in your 401(k) when you change jobs, your 401(k) plan could be automatically cashed out, which will trigger income tax and potentially the early withdrawal penalty on the amount distributed. However, you can avoid both of these situations by being proactive and moving your money out of the 401(k) plan to a retirement account of your own choosing. It can also be useful to open a 401(k) plan with an e-mail address and phone number that isn't tied to your job so that the 401(k) plan can continue to contact you when you no longer have access to the e-mail account and office phone line associated with your former job.

If you decide to move your money, make sure your account balance is transferred directly to the new retirement plan via a trustee-to-trustee transfer. If the check is made out to you, 20 percent of the balance will be withheld for income tax. You will then have sixty days to put the entire distribution, including the withheld 20 percent, into a new retirement account. If you don't meet the deadline you will have to pay income tax, and if you're under age fifty-five, an early withdrawal penalty on any amount that is not deposited in another retirement account. For example, if you have $5,000 in a 401(k) plan, your former employer will withhold $1,000 and give you a check for $4,000. In order to avoid paying income tax and the early withdrawal penalty, you will need to deposit that $4,000 and $1,000 from another source into another retirement account within sixty days. If you only put the $4,000 in a new 401(k) or IRA, the $1,000 that was withheld by your employer will be considered income that is subject to taxes and the early withdrawal penalty. You can avoid the withholding if you have the account balance directly paid to the trustee of the new plan.

Working for an Employer Without a 401(k)

If your employer doesn't offer a 401(k) plan, you're missing out on a huge opportunity to reduce your tax bill while saving for retirement. Savers who don't have access to a 401(k) account at work can contribute to an IRA, Roth IRA, or *my*RA, which offer tax perks similar to those of 401(k) plans, but the contribution limits are much lower. There's also no employer match on money you contribute to IRAs. You can accumulate additional savings in a taxable investment account, savings account, or certificate of deposit. Most savings accounts and certificates of deposit are insured by the Federal Deposit Insurance Corporation up to $250,000 per depositor in each participating bank, which means your savings is guaranteed not to decline in value. However, interest rates on these safe investments tend to be low. Investment accounts that hold stocks, bonds, and mutual funds have the potential to earn you higher returns, but they are not insured by the government, and you could lose money on these assets.

If you work for a small business with 100 or fewer employees, it's worth pointing out to your supervisor that the company might be eligible for a tax credit if it starts offering a 401(k) or similar type of retirement account to employees. The credit is worth 50 percent of the cost to set up and administer the plan, up to a maximum of $500 per year for each of the first three years of the plan. The company can claim the credit starting in the year before the plan begins.

Five Strategies to Boost Your 401(k) Balance

The tax breaks and employer contributions a 401(k) plan provides can help you increase your nest egg faster than you could on your own. But you also need to take care to avoid fees and penalties that will reduce your account balance. Try these strategies to grow your retirement savings:

1. Save Automatically

Set up your 401(k) contributions to be withheld from each paycheck, and aim to increase your savings rate once a year or each time you get a raise or bonus.

2. Get Employer Contributions

Finding a job with generous retirement benefits can help propel you to a secure retirement. If your employer's contributions are matching funds, take care to save enough in the 401(k) to qualify for the biggest possible payment for which you are eligible. Consider sticking around until you are vested in the 401(k) plan and can take the employer contributions with you when you leave.

3. Claim Tax Breaks

You can defer paying income tax on the money you contribute to a 401(k), and you don't have to pay income tax on the interest or investment earnings until you withdraw the money from the account. If you drop into a lower tax bracket in retirement, you will also lower your lifetime tax bill by saving in a 401(k).

4. Minimize Fees

401(k) fees are deducted from your retirement account balance. Choosing funds with low expense ratios will effectively boost the returns you earn on your investments. Take care to select the lowest-cost funds that meet your investment needs.

5. Avoid Penalties

There is a 10 percent early withdrawal penalty if you withdraw money from your 401(k) before age fifty-nine-and-a-half and a 50 percent penalty if you fail to begin withdrawing some of the money after age seventy-and-a-half. Both of these penalties can significantly reduce your retirement account balance if you don't take care to avoid them.

Catching Up When You're Behind

401(k) plans work best when you start saving in them early in your career. Even a small amount of savings can accumulate to an impressive amount if given enough time to compound. But a 401(k) plan can also be used to improve your retirement finances at the last minute, if you're willing to do some serious saving late in your career. If you committed to completely maxing out your 401(k) by contributing $24,000 per year between ages fifty and sixty-five and earn 7 percent annual returns, you will accumulate $625,728 after saving for fifteen years. Saving that much requires either a significant income or some sacrifices in other areas of your life, but it will greatly improve your finances later on in retirement.

STEP TAKEAWAYS

- Defer paying income tax on up to $18,000 by contributing to a 401(k) in 2016. If you're fifty or older, you can contribute as much as $24,000. Income tax won't be due on this money until it is withdrawn from the account.

- Avoid a 10 percent early withdrawal penalty by delaying 401(k) distributions until after age fifty-nine-and-a-half. But remember to begin taking withdrawals after age seventy-and-a-half to prevent an even bigger 50 percent penalty.

- Find out when you become vested in the 401(k) plan. You don't get to keep company contributions to your 401(k) until you are vested, which typically requires several years of job tenure. In some cases, staying at a job a little longer can be worth thousands of dollars.

- Determine what investment fees you are paying, and adjust your investment portfolio accordingly. Each 401(k) investment option in your plan charges different fees. Choosing low-cost funds will boost your returns.

- If you're changing jobs, consider rolling over your 401(k) balance directly from one financial institution to another. This can help you to avoid taxes and penalties when moving your money.

STEP 4
INVEST IN AN IRA

Individual retirement accounts (IRAs) allow you to claim a tax deduction on money you save for retirement. You can delay paying income tax on the money you deposit in an IRA and its investment earnings until you withdraw your savings from the account. Unlike 401(k) accounts, IRAs aren't tied to your job. You can continue to contribute to the same IRA your whole life, regardless of what company you currently work for.

Tax-deductible IRAs were created in 1974, and were initially only available to employees without pension plans at work. Workers were allowed to contribute as much as 15 percent of their pay up to a maximum of $1,500. A 1981 law expanded IRAs to all taxpayers with earned income, and increased the contribution limits to 100 percent of earnings or a maximum of $2,000. Income limits for participation were added in 1986, and have since been increased several times.

IRAs offer a wider selection of investments than 401(k) plans, and in many cases you can find an IRA that charges lower fees than your workplace retirement account. You can also roll over your 401(k) balance to an IRA each time you change jobs, which can make it simpler to manage your retirement portfolio. IRAs have slightly different rules than 401(k)s, and you need to carefully follow those rules to avoid penalties. Here's how to make optimum use of an IRA.

Make Sure You Qualify

You need income earned by working to save in an IRA. Wages, salaries, professional fees, bonuses, commissions, tips, and earnings from self-employment all count as income that you can contribute to an IRA. However, income from interest, dividends, rental properties, pensions, or annuities does not qualify you to make a tax-deductible IRA contribution. People age seventy-and-a-half and older are also no longer eligible to get a tax deduction for saving in a traditional IRA.

Maximize the Tax Benefits

IRAs have much lower contribution limits than 401(k)s. As of 2016 workers can contribute up to $5,500. Retirement savers age fifty and older can make catch-up contributions worth an additional $1,000 for a total of $6,500 per year. IRA contribution limits are not automatically adjusted each year to keep up with inflation. If you have more than one IRA, your contributions to all your IRAs cannot exceed these limits.

If a worker in the 25 percent tax bracket contributes $5,500 to an IRA, she will save $1,375 on her tax bill. Investors in the 15 percent tax bracket will save $825 on the same contribution, while those in the 28 percent bracket will save $1,540. A worker who is fifty or older and maxes out his IRA could reduce his tax bill by $975 if he's in the 15 percent tax bracket and $1,620 if he's in the 25 percent tax bracket. Income tax won't be due on IRA contributions until the money is withdrawn from the account.

Like 401(k) contributions, saving up to $2,000 in an IRA ($4,000 for couples) can qualify you for the saver's tax credit. If your adjusted gross income as an individual is below $30,750 ($46,125 for heads of household, and $61,500 for couples), your IRA contribution will qualify you for a tax credit worth between 10 percent and 50 percent of the amount saved.

FOR EXAMPLE

It's March, and Sally is getting ready to file her taxes. She enters all her income for the year into her tax planning software and arrives at the amount she owes. Sally is in the 25 percent tax bracket, and her tax bill is a little bit more than she would like to pay. The tax program she is using prompts her to enter any retirement account contributions she made. Sally doesn't have a 401(k) at work, and hasn't yet saved anything for retirement. But, just to see what would happen, Sally enters a $1,000 IRA contribution. This causes her tax bill to decrease by $250. Then Sally plugs in a $3,000 IRA contribution and $750 drops from her tax bill. Since Sally is age fifty, she can contribute a maximum of $6,500 to her IRA, which would remove $1,625 from her tax bill. Simply by moving some of her savings into an IRA, Sally can easily save over a thousand dollars on her tax bill. She won't owe income tax on her IRA contribution or the earnings until it is withdrawn from the account. And since she is already age fifty, Sally will only have to wait about nine more years, until age fifty-nine-and-a-half, until she can withdraw money from her IRA without incurring a 10 percent early withdrawal penalty.

Contribute to an IRA for Family Members

In addition to contributing to your own IRA, you can contribute to your spouse's IRA, even if he or she doesn't have any earned income. Once your children get a first part-time job, you could also contribute to an IRA in a child's name.

Spousal IRAs

You can double your tax savings if both you and your spouse contribute to an IRA. If you and your spouse both have compensation, you can each open your own IRA. You cannot open an IRA in both of your names. If only one spouse has compensation and you file a joint tax return, you can contribute $5,500 to an IRA in each spouse's name. Your combined contributions to your and your spouse's IRAs can be as much as $11,000. The limit climbs to $12,000 if one of you is age fifty or older and $13,000 if you both are age fifty or older. If you divorce, you cannot deduct any contributions to your spouse's IRA in that or a later year unless you remarry.

Open an IRA for Your Child or Grandchild

You don't have to be an adult to open an IRA, but you do need earned income. You could open an IRA in a child or grandchild's name once he or she gets a part-time job. If you put $1,000 in an IRA for a sixteen-year-old child and it earns 7 percent annual returns, it will be worth $27,530 when the child turns sixty-five without any additional contributions. Further, if you put that amount in a Roth IRA, there won't even be any tax to pay on that money in retirement. Since IRA balances are not considered in financial aid calculations, this type of saving will not impact your child's eligibility for federal financial aid for college unless the money is withdrawn from the account.

Meet the Contribution Deadline

IRA accounts have a later contribution deadline than 401(k) plans, which could allow you to reduce your tax bill shortly before filing your taxes. While 401(k) contributions are typically due by the end of the calendar year, you have until April 15 to make IRA contributions. When you are preparing your tax return, you can plug in a traditional IRA contribution to see how your tax bill will change. You might be able to reduce your tax bill by hundreds or even over a thousand dollars if you have the cash on hand and are able to deposit it in an IRA by your tax filing deadline.

If you make an IRA contribution between January 1 and April 15, take care to specify to which tax year you would like the contribution applied. If you don't indicate otherwise, the financial institution is allowed to apply an IRA contribution to the calendar year in which it was received. You can file a tax return claiming a tax deduction for a traditional IRA contribution before the money is in the account, as long as you make the contribution by April 15.

Contribute Your Tax Refund to an IRA

You can elect to have your income tax refund paid directly to your IRA. IRS form 8888, which you can download from *www.irs.gov/pub/irs-pdf/f8888.pdf*, allows you to directly deposit your tax refund into as many as three different saving or investment accounts, including IRAs.

In some years the deadline for IRA contributions changes slightly due to holidays. For example, April 18, 2016 is the IRA contribution deadline for tax-year 2015, due to the Emancipation Day holiday in the District of Columbia. And residents of Maine and Massachusetts have until April 19, 2016 to make 2015 IRA contributions due to the Patriots' Day holiday celebrated in those states. However, it's a good idea to submit your deposit at least a few days before the deadline to allow time for the contribution to be processed.

Watch Out for Income Limits

Employees who don't have access to a retirement account at work are eligible for a tax deduction on their IRA contribution no matter how much they earn. Employees who have 401(k)s can additionally save for retirement in an IRA. However, the tax deduction is phased out for investors who have a workplace retirement account such as a 401(k) and earn more than certain cutoffs. The tax deduction for traditional IRA contributions is phased out for those whose modified adjusted gross income is between $61,000 and $71,000 for individuals and $98,000 to $118,000 for couples in 2016. If you don't have a 401(k) or similar retirement account but are married to someone who does, the IRA contribution tax deduction is phased out if the couple's income is between $184,000 and $194,000 in 2016.

Who Can't Invest in an IRA

There are several groups of people who are prohibited from participating in IRAs. You can't save in an IRA if you don't have income that you earned through employment. You lose the ability to claim a tax deduction for a traditional IRA contribution if you have a 401(k) plan at work and your modified adjusted gross income exceeds $71,000 for individuals and $118,000 for couples. And people age seventy-and-a-half and older can't claim a tax deduction for traditional IRA contributions.

Make Saving Automatic

IRAs never have waiting periods before you can begin saving in the plan the way some 401(k) plans do. While there's no payroll withholding for IRAs, you can still automate your contributions by setting up a direct deposit to your IRA. Saving for retirement is easier for many people if the contributions happen automatically and don't require action every month.

If you contributed the maximum possible amount to an IRA account each year between 1975 and 2011 (a total of $99,500 in contributions, including catch-up contributions beginning in 2002) and invested it in an S&P 500 index fund, your balance would have grown to $729,508, according to Government Accountability Office calculations. But that amount would decline significantly if you took early withdrawals from the account or chose a more expensive investment option.

Avoid the Early Withdrawal Penalty

If you want to withdraw money from a traditional IRA before age fifty-nine-and-a-half, it is typically subject to a 10 percent early withdrawal penalty in addition to regular income tax on the amount withdrawn. However, there are a variety of ways to avoid the IRA early withdrawal penalty:

Medical Expenses

IRA distributions that are used to pay for unreimbursed medical expenses that exceed 10 percent of your adjusted gross income are not subject to the early withdrawal penalty.

Health Insurance

If you lose your job and collect unemployment compensation for twelve consecutive weeks following a job loss, you can take penalty-free IRA distributions to pay for health insurance for you, your spouse, and your dependents.

Disability

If you become disabled and can no longer work due to your physical or mental condition, distributions from your IRA will not be subject to the 10 percent penalty. But be prepared to prove it. The IRS says a physician must determine that your condition can be "expected to result in death or to be of long, continued, and indefinite duration."

Annuity Payments

If you set up a series of annuity payments over your life expectancy or the joint life expectancies of you and your spouse, they will not be subject to the early withdrawal penalty, even if you begin receiving the distributions before age fifty-nine-and-a-half. You must use an IRS-approved distribution method and take at least one withdrawal annually in order to receive this exception to the early withdrawal penalty.

College Costs

There is no early withdrawal penalty for IRA withdrawals used to pay for college costs including tuition, fees, books, supplies, and required equipment. Room and board also qualify for people who are at least half-time students. The education must be for you, your spouse, or the children or grandchildren of you or your spouse. However, it's important to note that IRA withdrawals are considered income and could reduce your eligibility for financial aid in future years.

First Home Purchase

You can withdraw up to $10,000 ($20,000 for couples) from an IRA without penalty to buy, build, or rebuild a first home. You qualify for the exemption if you haven't owned a home during the two years preceding the home purchase. This withdrawal can also be used for a first home purchase for a parent, child, or grandchild. The distribution must be used to pay home acquisition costs within 120 days. If the purchase or construction is canceled or delayed, you must put the money back in the IRA to continue to avoid the penalty.

Military Service

Members of the military reserves who take an IRA distribution during a period of active duty of more than 179 days do not have to pay a 10 percent penalty on the amount withdrawn. Qualifying organizations include the Army National Guard, Army Reserve, Naval Reserve, Marine Corps Reserve, Air National Guard, Air Force Reserve, and Coast Guard Reserve.

How Early Withdrawals Hurt Your Retirement Savings

These exceptions to the early withdrawal penalty can help you to feel more comfortable putting your money in an IRA, because you will know that you can get it back out if you need it for emergency or major life expenses. But being able to avoid the early withdrawal penalty doesn't mean you *should* pull money out of your IRA if it isn't absolutely necessary.

Even if you use the money for one of these IRS-sanctioned purposes, you will still need to pay income tax on each withdrawal. IRA contribution limits are just $5,500 per year, which makes it difficult to replace the money in the account. If you withdraw $20,000 from an IRA, it would take you four years to get that much money back into a tax-deferred account. And while the money is not in the account you are missing out on the tax-deferred growth.

Saving for Retirement versus College

When your income is limited, you may need to choose between saving for college for your children and saving for your own retirement. Most financial advisers say that saving for retirement should be your first priority. Children have a variety of options to pay for college including financial aid, student loans, and getting a part-time job. If you don't save enough for retirement and you don't receive a pension through your job, your only source of retirement income will be Social Security, which probably won't be enough on its own to provide a desirable retirement lifestyle.

However, if you do decide to use some of your retirement savings to help your children pay for college, watch out for penalties and fees while doing so. IRA withdrawals for college costs are exempt from the early withdrawal penalty, but you will still have to pay income tax on the distribution. If you're in the 25 percent tax bracket and withdraw $10,000 from an IRA for college tuition or expenses you will owe $2,500 in federal income tax on the distribution. You will pay less tax if you withdraw the money from a Roth IRA. Distributions from a Roth IRA that is at least five years old before you reach age fifty-nine-and-a-half will trigger income tax only on the portion of the withdrawal that comes from investment earnings.

You can also use 401(k) distributions for college costs, but unlike IRAs, the 10 percent early withdrawal penalty will apply if you're under age fifty-nine-and-a-half. A 401(k) distribution also triggers income tax, and you may be prohibited from making new contributions to the 401(k) plan for the six months following the distribution. Alternatively, you could borrow as much as 50 percent of your vested account balance up to $50,000 from your 401(k) plan rather than taking a distribution.

This strategy allows you to avoid any tax implications, but 401(k) loans for higher education expenses must be paid back with interest within five years. If you lose your job, the loan could become due sooner. Loans that aren't repaid are treated as distributions, and taxes and penalties then apply. It's a good idea to compare the terms of a 401(k) loan to other loans you might be eligible for including federal PLUS loans, home equity loans, and private education loans.

Withdrawals from 401(k)s and IRAs are considered income and could reduce the amount of federal financial aid for which your child qualifies. Waiting until your child's senior year of college or later to take a retirement account distribution can help prevent your offspring's financial aid package from being reduced. Also, you don't necessarily have to pay for your child's college costs up front. If your child qualifies for student loans, you can always help him or her pay them off later if you are in a better financial position then and your investments have had more time to grow.

Investment Selection

The financial institution that administers your 401(k) plan is chosen by your employer, but you get more choices with an IRA. You can open an IRA at:

- A bank or other financial institution
- A mutual fund company
- A life insurance company
- Through your stockbroker or an online broker

Compare all the options to see where you can build the lowest-cost portfolio.

IRAs offer nearly unlimited investment choices and significantly more options than 401(k) plans. However, you can't invest IRA funds in life insurance, collectibles, artwork, rugs, antiques, gems, metals, stamps, coins, or alcoholic beverages. If you use money in your IRA to purchase collectibles, that amount is considered a distribution in the year of the purchase, and taxes and the early withdrawal penalty could apply.

IRA trustees are permitted to impose additional restrictions on investments in IRAs they administer. While IRS law does not prohibit investing in real estate, some IRA trustees don't allow it because of administrative burdens. But: you are forbidden to buy property with your IRA for personal use. You also can't borrow money from your IRA or use it as security for a loan.

FOR EXAMPLE

Rob and Bob are both changing jobs. They each have $10,000 in a 401(k) account and plan to roll the entire balance over to an IRA.

Rob is busy at his new job and hasn't had time to set up an IRA. He elects to have the 401(k) balance distributed to him directly, thinking he will open up the IRA later. However, when he gets the check from his 401(k) plan, it's only for $8,000. The remaining $2,000, or 20 percent of the account balance, has been withheld for income tax. The following weekend he opens an IRA account and deposits the $8,000 he received. Rob doesn't put the remaining $2,000 in the IRA account within sixty days, because he never received it from his employer. When he files his taxes that year the $2,000 is considered a distribution, so he ends up having to pay 25 percent federal income tax, and, because he is fifty, he's also assessed a 10 percent early withdrawal penalty on that $2,000. The income tax and penalty end up costing him $700.

Bob has changed jobs before and already has an IRA. This time when he changes jobs, he has his 401(k) balance directly deposited from his 401(k) plan to the financial institution that administers his IRA. Since Bob has initiated a trustee-to-trustee transfer, there is no requirement that 20 percent be withheld for federal income tax. The entire 401(k) balance is rolled over to the IRA within a few days, and no taxes or penalties are triggered.

Rolling Money Over from a 401(k)

IRA accounts aren't tied to your job, which means you can continue to save in the same IRA as you switch employers. As indicated in a previous step, many people roll over the money in their 401(k) to an IRA each time they change jobs. IRA rollovers typically take place at a hectic time in your life: when you have been laid off, are starting a new job, or are beginning retirement. It's important to look at the fees charged by the IRA and each investment option within it. Compare the costs of several different IRAs to those of your 401(k) account, and look for one that charges reasonable fees on your investments.

An IRA rollover needs to be done carefully to avoid taxes and penalties. When you're moving money from a 401(k) to an IRA, a trustee-to-trustee transfer directly from one financial institution to another will help you to avoid tax withholding and the early withdrawal penalty. If the balance is distributed to you, 20 percent will be withheld for income tax. The entire amount that was in your 401(k) plan, including the withheld 20 percent, must be deposited in an IRA within sixty days or it will be considered a distribution. 401(k) distributions are taxed at your regular income tax rate and, if you are under age fifty-five, there is also a 10 percent early withdrawal penalty. If you only roll over part of your savings, income tax and potentially the early withdrawal penalty will be applied to any portion of your 401(k) balance that is not deposited in a new retirement account.

401(k)s versus IRAs

401(k)s and IRAs offer similar tax breaks, but they have different contribution limits and deadlines. Here are some of the important distinctions between 401(k)s and IRAs.

- **Contribution deadline.** 401(k) contributions typically need to be made before the end of the calendar year via payroll withholding, but you have until April 15 to make an IRA contribution that will qualify you for a tax deduction.

- **Contribution limits.** 401(k)s have much larger contribution limits than IRAs. Employees can defer paying income tax on as much as $18,000 in a 401(k), while the IRA contribution limit is $5,500.
- **Catch-up contributions.** Workers who are fifty and older can contribute an extra $6,000 to a 401(k). The catch-up contribution limit for IRAs is $1,000.
- **Early withdrawal penalty.** There's no longer a 10 percent early withdrawal penalty on IRA distributions taken after age fifty-nine-and-a-half. However, if you leave your job at age fifty-five or older, you can take distributions from your most recent 401(k) plan without incurring the early withdrawal penalty.
- **Age limits.** Once you turn seventy-and-a-half, you can no longer defer paying income tax on new traditional IRA contributions, but you can continue to save and claim a tax deduction on your 401(k) contributions.

STEP TAKEAWAYS

- By contributing to an IRA, you can defer paying income tax on up to $5,500, or $6,500 if you are age fifty or older.
- Spouses can contribute to an IRA in each of their names, even if one spouse doesn't work, which doubles their tax savings.
- The IRA contribution deadline is April 15, which means you can contribute shortly before filing your taxes to realize immediate savings on your current tax bill.
- IRA withdrawals used to pay for college won't trigger the early withdrawal penalty, but could reduce your child's eligibility for financial aid.
- You can take penalty-free withdrawals from your IRA before age fifty-nine-and-a-half for a variety of purposes including college costs, large medical bills, or a first home purchase.

STEP 5

ADD TAX DIVERSIFICATION WITH A ROTH ACCOUNT

Adding tax diversification to your portfolio gives you more control over how and when you pay taxes in retirement. In addition to traditional retirement accounts, you may want to consider putting money into Roth accounts. These don't give you a tax break up front, but the money grows without the drag of taxes, and withdrawals in retirement can be tax-free.

Roth IRAs were created by the Taxpayer Relief Act of 1997. The accounts are named after Senator William Roth Jr. of Delaware, who was an advocate for the bill. Since 2006, 401(k) plans have been allowed to amend their plans to add a Roth 401(k) option. Employers must establish a separate account for each participant who makes Roth contributions and keep that money separate from traditional 401(k) contributions because each type of account has different tax rules.

You have already paid income tax on contributions to Roth 401(k)s and Roth IRAs, so you don't have to worry about incurring a large tax bill in retirement, when you can least afford to pay it. While you don't get a tax break in the year you contribute to them, Roth accounts allow you to take tax-free distributions in retirement. You don't have to pay income tax on investment gains that accrue within your Roth accounts each year, and if you withdraw the money after age fifty-nine-and-a-half from an account that is at least five years old, you won't ever have to pay tax on your Roth IRA investment earnings. If you don't need the money, you don't have to take distributions from Roth IRAs at all during your lifetime. The earnings can continue to grow tax-free until you decide to withdraw the money, or you can use Roth accounts to pass on tax-free money to your heirs. You contribute after-tax dollars to Roth accounts, but the investment earnings aren't taxed while the money is in the account, and you can also take tax-free distributions from the account in retirement.

If you happen to need the money before retirement, the penalty for taking money out of a Roth account early is typically much smaller than the early withdrawal penalty on traditional retirement accounts. Here's how to lower your lifetime tax bill with Roth accounts.

Avoid Taxes in Retirement

When you save in a tax-deferred 401(k) or IRA, you are basically delaying paying taxes on your retirement savings until retirement. This can be beneficial if you drop into a lower tax bracket in retirement and pay a lower tax rate than you did while working. However, not everyone wants to be stuck with a tax bill in retirement when you could instead pay those taxes up front while you are working. You can't claim a tax deduction for your Roth account contributions, but distributions from the account, including the earnings, are often tax-free in retirement. (If you're not at least fifty-nine-and-a-half when you withdraw the money or if the account is not at least five years old you will suffer a tax penalty.)

Roth 401(k)s and IRAs have the same contribution limits as traditional 401(k)s and IRAs. You can save as much as $18,000 in a Roth 401(k) and $5,500 in a Roth IRA. Catch-up contributions of up to $1,000 to a Roth IRA and $6,000 to a Roth 401(k) are also allowed for those age fifty and older. You can contribute to both traditional and Roth accounts in the same year, as long as you don't exceed the contribution limits among all the retirement accounts you contribute to.

FOR EXAMPLE

Anna puts $5,000 in a traditional IRA at age thirty-five and then doesn't touch it or make any additional contributions. Since she is in the 25 percent tax bracket, she saves $1,250 on her tax bill the year she makes the contribution. The account earns 6 percent annual returns, on which she does not need to pay taxes each year. By the time Anna turns sixty-five, the IRA balance has grown to $28,717. Anna decides to withdraw 4 percent of the account balance each year, or about $1,149. Since Anna dropped into the lower 15 percent tax bracket in retirement, she can expect to pay about $4,308 in taxes on the money throughout her retirement. However, if she withdrew the entire balance at once and it pushed her into the higher 25 percent tax bracket, she would owe $7,179 in taxes.

Ava puts $5,000 in a Roth IRA at age thirty-five and also doesn't make any additional contributions. She doesn't get any tax breaks in the year she makes the contribution and pays $1,250 in income tax on that $5,000 as she earned it. The account earns 6 percent annual returns, with no income tax due on the gains, and grows to $28,717 by the time Ava turns sixty-five. Since Ava already paid income tax on her original $5,000 contribution and she waited until after age fifty-nine-and-a-half to take withdrawals, no income tax will be due on withdrawals from the account. Whether she withdraws the money as a lump sum or slowly throughout retirement will not impact her tax bill. She could also leave the money in the account to pass on tax-free savings to her beneficiary.

For example, if you saved $5,000 per year in a Roth IRA between ages fifty and sixty-five, you will have made $75,000 worth of contributions that you already paid tax on. If your account balance earned 7 percent annual returns it would grow to $134,440, $59,440 more than your contributions. Withdrawals from Roth accounts that are at least five years old and taken by account owners over age fifty-nine-and-a-half are tax-free. So, the account owner will not owe any tax on distributions, including the tax-free investment earnings of $59,440.

Although Roth 401(k) and Roth IRA contributions won't get you a tax deduction in the year you make the contribution, they can qualify you for the saver's tax credit. Those with modified adjusted gross incomes below $30,750 for individuals, $46,125 for heads of household, and $61,500 for couples in 2016 who save for retirement in a Roth account are eligible for the saver's credit. The credit is worth 10 percent to 50 percent of the amount contributed, up to $2,000 for individuals and $4,000 for couples.

Get a Roth 401(k) Match

If you elect to set up a Roth 401(k) account, your contributions to it will be separate from your traditional 401(k). Your employer may provide a match to your Roth 401(k) contributions, but the match won't be deposited in the after-tax Roth account, since company matching and profit-sharing contributions cannot be deposited in a Roth account. An employer can use Roth 401(k) contributions to calculate a 401(k) match, but all employer contributions must be allocated to a pre-tax traditional 401(k) account, even if they are matching money that was contributed to a Roth 401(k). You will owe income tax on the matching contributions and their earnings when you withdraw the money from your traditional 401(k).

How to Take a Tax-Free Distribution from a Roth Account

In order to take tax-free withdrawals from your Roth accounts, several conditions must be met. If the account is at least five years old and you are fifty-nine-and-a-half or older, no income tax will apply to Roth account distributions. If you suffer a disability or die, you or your heirs can also qualify for tax-free distributions from accounts that are five years old or older. If these conditions are not met, income tax and an early withdrawal penalty could be applied to part of your Roth account withdrawals.

Spousal Roth IRAs

You can contribute to a Roth IRA for your spouse based on your earned income. If you file a joint tax return, you can put up to $5,500 in a Roth IRA in your name and another $5,500 in a Roth IRA in your spouse's name. And if one or both of you is age fifty or older, you can contribute an extra $1,000 to a Roth IRA for each person over the age requirement. However, you cannot open a joint Roth IRA in both of your names. Roth 401(k)s can only be opened in the employee's name and do not permit contributions in a spouse's name.

Meet the Deadlines

Roth 401(k) contributions are typically due by the end of the calendar year. Your deposits can be automatically withheld from your paychecks throughout the year. Roth IRA contributions are due by your tax filing deadline, which is normally April 15 each year. You can set up a direct deposit from your paychecks or make the entire contribution at once. If you make a Roth IRA contribution between January 1 and April 15, you will need to specify which tax year you would like the contribution to be applied to.

Don't Exceed the Contribution Limits

If you deposit too much in a Roth IRA, there is a 6 percent excise tax applied to excess contributions. If you notice that you contributed too much, you can withdraw it and any earnings it generated before the due date of your tax return to avoid the penalty. Other ways to avoid the penalty include having the contribution returned to you within six months after the due date of your tax return and filing an amended return noting the change or applying the excess contribution to a later year.

Watch Out for Income Limits

You need earned compensation to contribute to a Roth IRA; this can include such things as wages, salaries, tips, professional fees, bonuses, commissions, or self-employment income. Income earned from investments or rental properties does not by itself make you eligible to contribute to an IRA. There are no income limits to participate in a Roth 401(k) account, but your ability to contribute to a Roth IRA is limited if you have a high income. You can contribute the full amount to a Roth IRA unless your income exceeds $117,000 for individuals and $184,000 for couples. Roth IRA eligibility is phased out for people whose modified adjusted gross income falls between $117,000 and $132,000 for individuals and $184,000 to $194,000 for married couples in 2016. People who earn more than that are not eligible to directly contribute to a Roth IRA. However, investors whose modified adjusted gross income exceeds these cutoffs may still be able to convert traditional IRA assets to a Roth IRA.

Convert to a Roth

High-income workers are restricted from directly contributing to Roth IRAs, but investors at any income level can convert all or part of their traditional IRA balance or 401(k) balance to a Roth IRA. Income tax will be due on the amount converted. For example, if you are in the 25 percent tax bracket and want to transfer $50,000 into a Roth IRA, you will owe $12,500 in income tax on the conversion. This maneuver works best when you pay the taxes with money from outside your retirement accounts so you don't end up with less money in retirement accounts after the rollover.

Converting a large amount can bump you into a higher tax bracket, increase your Medicare premiums, or reduce your child's eligibility for federal financial aid for college. However, you don't have to convert your entire traditional IRA account balance in a single year. You can space out the taxes by converting a small amount every year. Alternatively, you can do a Roth IRA conversion in a year when you have an unusually low income, such as when you are laid off, changing jobs, or otherwise didn't earn your usual salary.

Differences Between Roth IRAs and Roth 401(k)s

While Roth IRAs and Roth 401(k)s are both after-tax accounts that allow you to take tax-free distributions in retirement, there are several important differences between the two.

401(k)s Have Higher Contribution Limits

Roth 401(k)s have much larger contribution limits than Roth IRAs. Employees can save up to $18,000 in a Roth 401(k), and after age fifty they can make catch-up contributions worth an additional $6,000. Roth IRA contributions are limited to $5,500 and the limitation on catch-up contributions is $1,000.

IRAs Have a Later Contribution Deadline

Roth 401(k) contributions typically need to be made during the calendar year. You have until your tax filing deadline in April to make Roth IRA contributions.

Roth IRAs Have Income Limits

Workers with any amount of income can contribute to a Roth 401(k) if their employer offers one. However, your ability to save in a Roth IRA is limited if your modified adjusted gross income exceeds $117,000 for individuals and $184,000 for couples and prohibited once your income surpasses $132,000 for individuals and $194,000 for couples as of 2016. Workers with higher incomes may still be eligible to convert traditional IRA assets to a Roth.

Roth 401(k)s Require Withdrawals in Retirement

Roth 401(k)s typically require account owners to take annual distributions from the account after age seventy-and-a-half, while Roth IRAs have no withdrawal requirements for the original account owner.

Protect Your Roth Accounts When Changing Jobs

When you leave a job with a Roth 401(k) plan, you can choose to leave the money in your former employer's plan if the balance is over $5,000, or you can roll the balance over to a new employer's Roth 401(k) or a Roth IRA. Rollovers into another Roth 401(k) are only allowed via a direct rollover to the new employer's plan.

When you roll over a Roth 401(k) to a new Roth IRA, the five-year waiting period before you can take tax-free distributions from a Roth IRA starts over. However, if you roll over a Roth 401(k) to an existing Roth IRA, the five-year period is measured from your earlier contributions. If you roll over your retirement savings from one Roth IRA to another Roth IRA, the five-year period used to determine tax-free distributions does not change. The five-year period begins with the first year that contributions were made to the original Roth IRA.

More Flexibility

Roth IRAs give you additional flexibility to make contributions and withdrawals from your retirement accounts throughout your lifetime. Roth IRAs don't have age restrictions the way traditional IRAs do. While traditional IRAs prohibit people over age seventy-and-a-half from saving in the account, you can make contributions to a Roth IRA regardless of your age. Furthermore, you are not required to take distributions from Roth IRAs as long as you live, which gives you the ability to withdraw the money only when you need it. However, distributions from Roth 401(k)s are required after age seventy-and-a-half, unless you're still working and don't own 5 percent or more of the company you work for.

Roth accounts also allow you to maximize the amount of money you can store in tax-sheltered accounts. Money you have in a traditional 401(k) or IRA doesn't completely belong to you, because you still owe taxes on it. But you have already paid income tax on the money in your Roth accounts using funds outside of your retirement accounts, which means the money in your Roth account gives you more spending power. If you have $1 million in a Roth account, you are truly a millionaire. If you have $1 million in a traditional retirement account and you are in the 25 percent tax bracket, you really only have $750,000 that you can spend in retirement. All the funds in your Roth IRA will be available to use for expenses in retirement.

Easier Early Access to Your Money

If you think you might need access to your retirement savings before retirement, it's less expensive to withdraw the money from a Roth account than a traditional retirement account. There's a 10 percent early withdrawal penalty applied to most IRA distributions before age fifty-nine-and-a-half. However, for early Roth distributions you will only owe income tax and the early withdrawal penalty on the portion of the withdrawal that comes from investment earnings. Roth IRAs also have the same exceptions to the early withdrawal penalty as traditional IRAs, including a first home purchase, higher education expenses, unreimbursed medical costs, and health insurance costs while unemployed.

When you withdraw money early from a Roth IRA, your nontaxable contributions will be distributed before any of your taxable earnings. So, as long as you don't withdraw more than the amount you contributed to the account, you could avoid paying tax on the distribution. However, early withdrawals from Roth 401(k)s are prorated between nontaxable Roth contributions and taxable earnings. A portion of an early Roth

401(k) withdrawal is likely to be taxable. Alternatively, you can take a loan from a Roth 401(k) if your plan allows it.

Fewer Taxes for Heirs

You can use Roth IRAs to leave money to your children or grandchildren. Traditional IRAs require you to take regular withdrawals in retirement, and your heirs will need to pay taxes on any money left to them as they withdraw it. Roth 401(k)s also require withdrawals during retirement. However, you can leave money in a Roth IRA throughout your lifetime, and no distributions are required in retirement. If there is money left in the account after you pass away, your heirs may be able to receive tax-free distributions from the account.

FOR EXAMPLE

Ted and Tom both hope to leave some of their retirement savings to their heirs, but they go about it in different ways.

Ted contributes $5,000 to a traditional IRA at age fifty-five and names his daughter as the beneficiary of the account. Since Ted is in the 25 percent tax bracket, he saves $1,250 in federal taxes by putting the money in the account. When Ted passes away at age seventy, the account is worth $11,983. Ted's daughter Tess can choose to withdraw the entire $11,983 and pay the resulting income tax bill of $2,996, or she can take smaller withdrawals throughout her lifetime and pay tax on each withdrawal.

Tom puts $5,000 in a Roth IRA at age fifty-five and designates his son Tim as the beneficiary. Tom has already paid income tax on this $5,000 and doesn't get a tax break for his contribution. When Tom passes away at seventy, Tim inherits the now $11,983 in the account. Tim will be required to withdraw the balance from the Roth account, but income tax will not be due on the distribution.

Roths versus Traditional Retirement Accounts

To decide which type of retirement account is best for you, you need to compare your current tax rate to an estimate of what you think your tax rate will be in retirement. If you are earning a good income now and expect to drop into a lower tax bracket in retirement, it's often better to take the tax break while you are working by contributing to a traditional retirement account. But if you think your tax rate will be higher in retirement than it is now, you will lower your lifetime tax bill by saving for retirement in a Roth account. Contributing to a Roth account is often an especially good deal for people who are in a low tax bracket now but expect to move into a higher one later on in life. In addition, when your money is in a Roth IRA you don't have to worry about the possibility of higher tax rates in the future because you won't owe taxes on the money when it is withdrawn.

You can hedge your bets about future tax rates by saving some money for retirement in both types of accounts. You can contribute up to $18,000 to either type of 401(k) and $5,500 to either type of IRA in 2016, as long as your total contributions to both types of accounts do not exceed these limits. If you are age fifty or older, the contribution limits jump to $24,000 for 401(k)s and $6,500 for IRAs. If you save in a Roth 401(k) and your employer match or other company contributions are provided in a traditional 401(k), you will automatically be saving in accounts with two different tax treatments.

Differences Between Traditional and Roth IRAs

To recap: Roth IRAs have the same contribution limits as traditional IRAs, but there are a couple of important differences between the two accounts:

- **No tax deduction for Roth contributions.** You cannot deduct Roth IRA contributions from your taxable income the way you can claim a tax deduction on deposits in a traditional IRA.
- **No age restrictions on Roth IRAs.** While people over age seventy-and-a-half are prohibited from continuing to make contributions to traditional IRAs and are required to take annual withdrawals from the account, older workers can continue to save in Roth IRAs and there are no withdrawal requirements in retirement.
- **Roth distributions can be tax-free.** Distributions from Roth IRAs that are at least five years old are tax-free in retirement if the account owner is over age fifty-nine-and-a-half. However, income tax will be due on all traditional IRA withdrawals.

Tax Diversification

Putting some of your retirement money in pre-tax accounts and some in after-tax accounts adds tax diversification to your portfolio. While income tax will be due on each withdrawal from traditional 401(k)s and traditional IRAs, no income tax is due on withdrawals from Roth 401(k)s and Roth IRAs after age fifty-nine-and-a-half from accounts that are at least five years old. The savings you keep in a Roth account can help you control your tax bill in retirement. For example, if you wanted to stay in a low tax bracket, you could withdraw an amount from your taxable retirement accounts sufficient to keep you in a low tax bracket and then withdraw the rest of the income you need to meet your expenses from a Roth IRA, which will not be taxable.

Such diversification will give you options in retirement. Here are five reasons to diversify some of your retirement savings into a Roth account:

1. **Tax-free investment growth.** The money in your Roth account grows without the drag of taxes each year. And if you delay

withdrawals until after age fifty-nine-and-a-half and the account is at least five years old, you won't ever have to pay tax on the investment gains in your Roth IRA.

2. **Tax-free withdrawals in retirement.** You owe income tax on each withdrawal from a traditional 401(k) or IRA. Distributions from Roth accounts in retirement are often tax-free.

3. **Less costly early withdrawals.** If you need access to your retirement savings while you are still working, the taxes and penalties will typically be less costly if you take the early distribution from a Roth account because you will owe income tax and the early withdrawal penalty only on the portion of the withdrawal that comes from the investment earnings.

4. **Retirement flexibility.** Distributions from traditional 401(k)s, Roth 401(k)s, and traditional IRAs are required each year after age seventy-and-a-half. But Roth IRAs don't have distribution requirements in retirement, and the money in the account can continue to grow tax-free for as long as you live.

5. **Pass tax-free money on to heirs.** Your children or grandchildren will be stuck with the tax bill for money you bequeath to them in a traditional 401(k) or IRA. However, your heirs will be able to take tax-free distributions from the Roth IRA you leave to them.

The *My*RA

The U.S. Department of the Treasury recently created a new type of retirement account, the *my*RA, which was announced by President Barack Obama during his State of the Union address in 2014. This account is guaranteed by the government never to decline in value, and doesn't have any fees or minimum balance requirements.

The *my*RA is designed for people who don't have a 401(k) or similar type of retirement account at work. All contributions to *my*RAs are invested in a U.S. Treasury savings bond. The investment earns a variable interest rate and had an average annual return of 3.19 percent over the ten-year period from December 2004 to December 2014. Participants can save up to $15,000 in a *my*RA and keep that account for as long as thirty years, after which the account balance will be rolled over to a private-sector Roth IRA. *My*RAs can be funded by direct deposit through an employer, but companies do not administer or contribute to the accounts. You can also set up one-time or recurring contributions from a checking or savings account or redirect a portion of your federal tax refund to the account. To be eligible to participate in a *my*RA, workers must earn less than $131,000 for individuals and $193,000 for married couples.

The tax treatment of a *my*RA is similar to a Roth IRA. After-tax dollars are contributed to *my*RAs. Savers can contribute up to $5,500 per year, or $6,500 if they are age fifty or older. Contributions can be withdrawn tax-free at any time. The interest can be withdrawn without penalty once the account is at least five years old and the saver reaches age fifty-nine-and-a-half. Contributions to a *my*RA can also qualify you for the saver's credit. You can open an account at *https://myra.gov*.

STEP TAKEAWAYS

- When you contribute after-tax dollars to a Roth 401(k) or Roth IRA, they can be withdrawn tax-free after age fifty-nine-and-a-half from accounts that are at least five years old.

- You are not required to take withdrawals from Roth IRAs in retirement, but Roth 401(k) distributions are required after age seventy-and-a-half.

- One way to determine which type of IRA or 401(k) you should use is to compare your current tax rate to what you expect your tax rate to be in retirement. If you expect to pay higher taxes later, a Roth IRA or a Roth 401(k) allows you to lock in today's low tax rate.

- You can add tax diversification to your retirement portfolio by splitting your savings between both Roth IRAs and traditional IRAs.

- The *my*RA is a new type of Roth retirement account that is guaranteed by the government never to lose value.

STEP 6

MINIMIZE TAXES BEFORE AND AFTER RETIREMENT

The tax code has a variety of incentives to encourage retirement savers. Retirement accounts allow you to reduce your tax bill when you set money aside for retirement. You can claim a tax deduction on your 401(k) and IRA contributions, or use a Roth account to prepay taxes so you can take tax-free withdrawals in retirement. And low-income workers can additionally claim the saver's credit on their retirement account contributions.

However, at some point you will have to pay tax on your retirement savings. If you choose to defer taxes on your retirement savings during your working years, you will need to take care to minimize your tax bill when taking distributions from your retirement accounts. The timing of withdrawals from your traditional retirement account, Roth account, or taxable accounts impacts what your tax bill will be in retirement. Using all three types of accounts gives you a measure of control over how much tax you will pay each year. Paying attention to how various sources of retirement income are taxed could save you a significant amount of money in retirement.

Seven Ways to Minimize Taxes While Saving for Retirement

Putting money in a 401(k) or IRA qualifies you for tax perks, even as the money grows on your behalf for retirement. Here's how much you can put into each type of account, and other strategies to use retirement accounts to reduce your tax bill:

401(k)

As of 2016 you can defer paying income tax on up to $18,000 that you contribute to a traditional 401(k). As discussed earlier, income tax won't be due on your contributions until you withdraw the money.

IRA

Savers can claim a tax deduction on up to $5,500 that is deposited in a traditional IRA in 2016. You will need to pay income tax on each distribution.

Roth 401(k)

Depositing up to $18,000 in a Roth 401(k) won't get you a tax break in the year you make the contribution, but you typically won't have to pay tax on the withdrawals in retirement.

Roth IRA

Contributing up to $5,500 in after-tax dollars to a Roth IRA will create an opportunity to earn tax-free growth and take tax-free distributions in retirement.

Catch-up Contributions

Workers age fifty and older can contribute an additional $6,000 to a 401(k) and $1,000 to an IRA as catch-up contributions. However, you can no longer contribute to a traditional IRA after age seventy-and-a-half.

FOR EXAMPLE

Jane and Jack are a married couple who earn $35,000, and are beginning to build a nest egg for retirement. They managed to put $4,000 into an IRA. Since they are in the 15 percent tax bracket, their $4,000 IRA contribution reduces their tax bill by $600. Due to their modest income, the couple also qualifies for the saver's credit, which in their case is worth 50 percent of the amount they deposit in a retirement account, or $2,000. So, Jane and Jack's $4,000 IRA contribution only cost them $1,400 after factoring in their tax deduction and credit.

Bruce and Betty earn slightly more than Jane and Jack, bringing in $38,000. They also save $4,000 in an IRA and get a tax deduction worth $600 for their retirement account contribution. However, due to their slightly higher income, Bruce and Betty's saver's credit is worth 20 percent of the amount they contribute to an IRA, or $800. So, Bruce and Betty's $4,000 IRA contribution costs them $2,600.

Saver's Credit

Retirement savers with incomes below $30,750 for singles, $46,125 for heads of household, and $61,500 for married couples in 2016 can claim the saver's credit in addition to the tax deduction on their 401(k) and IRA contributions. The credit is worth 10 percent to 50 percent of the amount saved in a retirement account, up to $2,000 for individuals and $4,000 for couples.

Save Your Tax Refund

You can have part or all of your tax refund directly deposited into an IRA using IRS form 8888, which will allow you to reduce your tax bill and boost your retirement savings at the same time.

The Order of Saving

With so many retirement account choices, it can be difficult to know where to begin. You will obviously get the biggest possible tax break if you contribute the maximum allowed amount to each retirement account for which you qualify. If you completely max out a tax-deferred 401(k) and IRA, you could defer paying income tax on $23,500. Those age fifty and older can defer paying income tax on as much as $30,500 if they qualify for both a 401(k) and an IRA. However, few people earn enough to funnel that much cash into retirement accounts each year.

If your financial resources are more limited, you need to choose the best place to save. Your first priority should be to get any 401(k) match offered by your employer. Employer-matching contributions are the best possible return you can get on an investment. For example, if your employer contributes 50 cents for each dollar you save in the 401(k) plan, that's a 50 percent gain on the money you save, and on top of that you get a tax break and investment gains.

Once you have gotten the maximum possible employer contribution, then you can choose to save more in your employer's 401(k) plan or contribute to an IRA or Roth IRA. There are several factors to consider when making this decision. You can compare the investment options offered in your 401(k) plan to an IRA, and choose the account that has lower fees and is likely to produce a higher return. Also, if your employer only offers a traditional 401(k), you can also save in a Roth IRA to add tax diversification to your portfolio. Saving for retirement in traditional and Roth retirement accounts gives you options in retirement to control how much you will pay in taxes each year. You can time your withdrawals from each type of account to minimize your overall tax bill. Once you max out your IRA or Roth IRA contributions, you will need to continue saving in your employer's plan if you want to get additional tax breaks for your retirement saving.

It's also important to do some saving outside of retirement accounts. Regular saving and investment accounts don't offer tax perks for contributing, and you will likely have to pay taxes on the gains each year. However, these accounts are also more accessible for everyday expenses or emergencies because there aren't any penalties for withdrawing the money before a certain age or requirements that you have to withdraw the money by a particular age.

Choose Low-Tax Investments

Different types of investments are taxed at different rates. The type of account the investment is in also impacts your tax rate. You can lower your tax bill by carefully selecting the type of account for each investment.

Every investment in your traditional retirement account will be taxed at the same rate (your regular income-tax rate) when you withdraw the money from the account, regardless of what your money was invested in inside the 401(k) plan. So retirement accounts are good places to keep investments that would be taxed at your regular tax rate, such as most types of government and corporate bonds.

Investments held outside of your retirement accounts are taxed at different rates depending on the type of investment. Some types of investment returns are taxed at a lower rate than your regular income-tax rate. If your portfolio has both tax-sheltered and taxable investment accounts, you can lower your tax bill by holding investments with especially low tax rates in your taxable account and putting investments taxed at regular rates in your 401(k) or IRA.

Great Investments for Taxable Accounts

While the following investments can be held within a retirement account, there is a tax perk available if they are held outside of your retirement accounts.

- **Municipal bonds.** State and local governments issue municipal bonds to finance infrastructure or other local projects. Bondholders receive interest payments that are exempt from federal and sometimes state and local taxation. There's no need to put municipal bonds in a retirement account, because you are already getting a tax break on the investment. Bonds, particularly government-issued ones, are generally considered safer investments than stocks, since they will fail only if the issuer defaults.

- **Investments that generate long-term capital gains.** If you hold a stock for more than one year before you sell it, your capital gain or loss is considered long-term. Long-term capital gains are taxed at a much lower rate than short-term gains and your ordinary income. The tax rate on most net capital gains is no higher than 15 percent for most taxpayers (although it can be 20 percent for people with very high incomes). Mutual funds can also generate capital gains distributions that are taxed at the long-term capital gains rate. If you hold investments that generate long-term capital gains in your 401(k) or IRA you don't need to report losses or gains on your tax return while the money is in the account, and you can defer paying tax on it until you withdraw the money. But when you do withdraw the money, it will be taxed at your ordinary tax rate instead of the typically lower long-term capital gains tax rate.

Great Investments for Retirement Accounts

The following investments are subject to high tax rates, which makes retirement accounts the ideal place to stash them.

Treasury Inflation-Protected Securities (TIPS)

These securities are indexed to inflation in order to shield you from its effects. They are generally considered low-risk. Interest payments from Treasury Inflation-Protected Securities, and increases in the principal of TIPS, are subject to federal tax, but exempt from state and local income taxes. It's particularly important to hold TIPS in an IRA, because you are taxed each time the principal value of these bonds rises to keep pace with inflation, even if your TIPS hasn't matured and you haven't yet received a payment of principal. A retirement account can shield you from the annual tax bill until you are ready to distribute the money.

Bonds

Corporate and government bonds and bond funds, with the exception of municipal bonds, are often great candidates for your retirement accounts. Interest from bonds and money market funds is taxed as ordinary income. Keeping bonds in your retirement account allows you to defer tax until you withdraw the money from the account.

Investments That Generate Short-Term Capital Gains

Capital gains on investments that are sold within a year of purchasing them are considered short-term. If you plan to actively trade stocks, you might rack up short-term gains but could defer paying tax on them in a retirement account. It's best to hold investments that distribute short-term capital gains in a 401(k) or IRA.

Drawing Down Your Retirement Savings

While it's important to get money into retirement accounts, you also need to be able to get it back out without paying an excessive tax bill. If you have amassed a significant nest egg and aren't careful, taxes could become one of your biggest retirement expenses. The money that wasn't taxed on its way into a retirement account will be taxed on its way out. The catch of tax-deferred retirement accounts is that you will owe tax on that money in retirement, at a time when you are trying to make your existing savings last as long as possible.

The money you have in tax-deferred 401(k)s and IRAs doesn't completely belong to you. You have to pay tax on each withdrawal. So, having $1 million in an IRA doesn't make you a millionaire. You actually have $850,000, if you can manage to withdraw all the money while staying in the 15 percent tax bracket. If the money you withdraw is taxed at the 25 percent rate, your $1 million IRA is only worth $750,000 after taxes. If you have a large traditional 401(k) or IRA balance, sometimes spacing out withdrawals over a greater number of years—perhaps beginning to withdraw some of the money in your sixties instead of waiting until your seventies—can help you to pay a lower tax rate.

Roth 401(k)s and Roth IRAs that are at least five years old are useful to own in retirement because the withdrawals are not taxed. You can withdraw as much as you need to without worrying about incurring a large tax bill.

There aren't any tax perks for saving in regular savings and investment accounts, and you will need to pay taxes on the interest or investment gains each year. However, these accounts offer easier access to your money for everyday spending or emergencies. There are no penalties for withdrawing your money before a certain age or withdrawal requirements in retirement.

Taking Required Minimum Distributions from 401(k)s and IRAs

Traditional 401(k)s and individual retirement account contributions earn you a valuable tax deduction during your working years. But in retirement you need to start withdrawing the money from your retirement accounts and pay income tax on it.

Required minimum distribution rules are designed to encourage withdrawals during the lifetime of the original account owner and his or her spouse. Withdrawals are required to discourage the use of tax-deferred retirement accounts as a vehicle to leave money to heirs. You also need to be aware that there are additional distribution rules for inherited retirement accounts.

If you have accumulated a large retirement account balance, the tax on required minimum distributions can be a major retirement expense. However, you can minimize the income tax you pay if you are strategic about how you take your distributions. Here's how to reduce the income tax bill for your retirement account withdrawals.

Take Distributions on Time

Withdrawals from traditional IRAs and 401(k)s are required after age seventy-and-a-half, and you must pay income tax on each withdrawal. The penalty for missing a required minimum distribution or withdrawing the incorrect amount is 50 percent of the amount that should have been withdrawn, in addition to the regular income tax.

Your first required minimum distribution must be taken by April 1 of the year after you turn seventy-and-a-half. If you turned seventy-and-a-half in 2015, your first required minimum distribution is due by April 1, 2016. You must take subsequent required minimum distributions by December 31 each year. If you delay your first required minimum distribution until April, you will need to take two required minimum distributions in the same year, which could result in an abnormally high tax bill.

Investors who continue to work in retirement may be able to delay required minimum distributions from a 401(k), but not from an IRA. If you are employed and don't own 5 percent or more of the company you work for, you can postpone withdrawals from your current 401(k) plan until you actually retire, if your plan allows it. However, IRA withdrawals and distributions from 401(k)s associated with previous jobs will continue to be required.

While 401(k) and IRA distributions aren't required until after age seventy-and-a-half, some people elect to start taking them earlier in order to pay a lower tax rate on each distribution. If you have a large retirement account balance, it can make sense to begin taking withdrawals from your retirement accounts at a younger age so you can space out the withdrawals over more years and potentially pay a lower tax rate on each distribution.

Withdraw the Correct Amount

You must calculate 401(k) distributions and take them separately from each 401(k) account. IRA accounts also require you to calculate the required minimum distribution separately for each IRA, but you can withdraw the total amount from any IRA or combination of IRAs.

Required minimum distributions are calculated by dividing your 401(k) balance by an IRS estimate of your life expectancy. Sometimes a spouse's age is also taken into account. 401(k) account owners can take several distributions throughout the year as long as the minimum required amount is met by December 31 (or April 1 for the first distribution). You can withdraw more than the required amount, but the excess amount cannot be used to satisfy a future year's required minimum distribution.

Rolling Over to an IRA

Some workers choose to roll their 401(k) balance over to an IRA each time they change jobs or in retirement. There can be benefits to doing this, including reducing the number of accounts you need to keep track of and accessing a wider variety of investment options. Also, some IRAs have lower fees than high-cost 401(k) plans.

However, there are a couple of specific circumstances when it makes sense to keep your money in a 401(k) plan. If you retire

FOR EXAMPLE

At age seventy-five, Sal is enjoying a very active retirement, and he forgot to take a $5,000 required minimum distribution from a traditional IRA. There is a 50 percent tax penalty for skipping a required minimum distribution, and the penalty is applied in addition to the income tax due on the withdrawal. Since he's in the 25 percent tax bracket, Sal's forgotten $5,000 required IRA withdrawal results in him owing $3,750 in taxes and penalties. He will get to keep only $1,250 of the distribution. If Sal had remembered to take the $5,000 withdrawal before the end of the calendar year he would have gotten $3,750 after paying income tax on the distribution.

Saul turned seventy-and-a-half in 2014, which is an important age for retirement planning. His first required minimum distribution from a traditional IRA is due by April 1 of the year after he turns seventy-and-a-half. Since Saul wants to defer paying income tax on his savings for as long as possible, he takes his first $5,000 withdrawal in March 2015. Saul's second required distribution, another $5,000, is due by December 31, 2015, and he takes it in December. IRA withdrawals count as income, and Saul's retirement income puts him close to the cutoff between the 15 and 25 percent tax brackets. On the first $5,000 IRA withdrawal, Saul paid the 15 percent tax rate, or $750 in income tax on the distribution. However, the second IRA distribution pushes him up into the 25 percent tax bracket, and he ends up paying $1,250 in income tax on the second distribution. If Saul had instead taken his first $5,000 IRA distribution in 2014 and his second $5,000 distribution in 2015, he could have paid the 15 percent income tax rate on both distributions.

between ages fifty-five and fifty-nine, you will be able to take penalty-free withdrawals from the 401(k) plan from your most recent job, but if you roll that money over to an IRA you will have to wait until age fifty-nine-and-a-half to avoid the 10 percent early withdrawal penalty.

If you plan to work past age seventy-and-a-half, you may be able to continue to delay distributions from your 401(k) account, but IRA distributions will be required to avoid a 50 percent penalty. Company stock also gets special tax treatment when held in an employer-sponsored 401(k). When you withdraw company stock from the 401(k) plan, the sale may qualify for the long-term capital gains tax rate of 15 percent, but if you roll the company stock over to an IRA the appreciation will be taxed at the typically higher ordinary income-tax rate upon withdrawal.

Distributions from Roth Accounts

You are required to take withdrawals from Roth 401(k) accounts beginning after age seventy-and-a-half. However, if you are still working for a company you don't have an ownership stake in, you can delay withdrawals from your Roth 401(k) until you actually retire. Withdrawals from Roth 401(k)s that are at least five years old will not be taxed if you're over age fifty-nine-and-a-half. You are not required to withdraw money from a Roth IRA during your lifetime.

If you withdraw money from a Roth account before it is five years old you may have to pay tax on a portion of the distribution. The five-year period in which you could be taxed begins on the first day of the year in which you begin to contribute to the Roth account. The amount that you contribute to the account is not considered income or taxed, even if you withdraw it in the first five years you own the account. But the earnings the account generates could be taxable if you withdraw the money before the account is five years old and you reach age fifty-nine-and-a-half.

Roth IRAs and Roth 401(k)s treat early withdrawals differently. When you take an early distribution from an IRA, your nontaxable contributions are withdrawn before any of your taxable earnings. If you withdraw an amount equal to or less than the amount you contributed to the account, the distribution won't be taxable. However, early withdrawals from Roth 401(k)s are prorated between your Roth contributions and earnings. So, a portion of an early Roth 401(k) withdrawal is likely to be taxable.

The taxable portion of a Roth 401(k) distribution is calculated by multiplying the amount you withdrew by the ratio of Roth contributions you made to the total account balance. For example, if you withdraw $5,000 from a Roth account to which you contributed $9,400 and the account accumulated $600 in investment gains, $4,700 of the withdrawal is not taxable and $300 will be taxed as income.

If you roll over a Roth 401(k) to a new Roth IRA, the five-year period when earnings are taxable starts over again. However, if you roll over your Roth 401(k) to an existing Roth IRA, the five-year taxable period is measured from the earlier contribution. So, if you are over age fifty-nine-and-a-half and the earlier contribution was made more than five years ago, you could withdraw your most recent rollover without paying tax on it. To make sure your retirement distributions from Roth accounts will be completely tax-free, take care to set up an account five or more years before you would like to take distributions.

Inheriting an IRA

Inheriting an IRA typically occurs during one of the worst moments in your life: a loved one has passed away. But even during this challenging time you will need to pay attention to some rules and deadlines if you want to avoid taxes and penalties on the gift your family member entrusted to you.

If you inherit an IRA from your spouse, you get the option to treat it as your own IRA by designating yourself as the new owner or rolling it over into your own IRA. Treating the IRA as your own allows you to continue to defer paying taxes on the inherited IRA until you withdraw the money. Spouses can also elect to treat themselves as a beneficiary of the inherited account, which allows them to begin withdrawing the money without incurring the early withdrawal penalty, even if they are under age fifty-nine-and-a-half. If the account owner died before turning seventy-and-a-half, distributions to the spouse do not need to begin until the year the owner would have reached age seventy-and-a-half. If you take a distribution from a deceased spouse's IRA and then change your mind about it, you can put it into your own IRA within sixty days before it becomes a taxable distribution.

If you inherit an IRA from someone other than your spouse, you are considered a beneficiary. If the deceased owner of the IRA has been taking required minimum distributions from the account, you must continue with that distribution schedule until the end of the calendar year if he or she had not already taken it. Income tax will be due on each traditional IRA withdrawal.

In the year after the account owner's death, you need to recalculate the new required minimum distribution based on your or the original account owner's life expectancy—whichever is longer. If the original owner of the IRA passed away before taking any required distributions from the account, the distributions can be calculated using your life expectancy or distributed at any time over a period of five years. The method you use to withdraw the money from the account will impact how much tax is due because each withdrawal will be taxed as income. If you fail to take appropriate distributions from the account you will owe a 50 percent tax on the amount that should have been withdrawn, in addition to owing the regular income tax.

If an IRA account has multiple beneficiaries, the age of the oldest person inheriting the account is used to calculate the required minimum distributions from the account. Alternatively, the IRA can be split into separate accounts for each person who inherited the IRA. Splitting up the account can help younger beneficiaries to reduce their distribution requirements and the resulting tax bill. Younger beneficiaries will be able to take out smaller distributions each year due to their longer life expectancy.

Three Tips
Distributions

Traditional, Roth, and inherited retirement accounts have different withdrawal requirements and tax treatments. Make sure you pay attention to these deadlines and requirements:

1. Withdrawals from traditional IRAs, traditional 401(k)s, and Roth 401(k)s are required after age seventy-and-a-half. You are not required to withdraw money from your Roth IRA during your lifetime.
2. Income tax will be due on traditional 401(k) and IRA withdrawals, but you won't have to pay any tax on withdrawals after age fifty-nine-and-a-half from Roth accounts that are at least five years old.
3. You are required to take distributions and pay any resulting tax bill from inherited IRAs, unless you inherit an IRA from a spouse. Spouses have the option to roll an inherited IRA into their own IRA.

Use a Smart Draw-Down Strategy

Taking distributions from a 401(k) or IRA means you need to pay tax on that money, but you don't have to spend it. You can put the money in a savings or investment account and continue to earn interest on it.

A conservative draw-down strategy involves spending 3–4 percent of your portfolio each year in retirement, and perhaps adjusting that amount to keep up with inflation. Your portfolio includes both your retirement and taxable investment accounts. If you had a starting balance of $100,000, that means you would withdraw $4,000 the first year, and then slightly more the next year depending on inflation.

A Congressional Research Service analysis calculated that a draw-down rate of 4 percent on an investment portfolio with 35 percent U.S. stocks and 65 percent corporate bonds would be 89.4 percent likely to last thirty-five years or more. Retirees who want to further reduce their risk of running out of money in retirement could amend this strategy to withdraw slightly less when their investments perform poorly to help them recover. But this strategy won't work if you will be tempted to spend more than 4 percent of your savings each year or are forced to use some of your retirement money for an emergency.

The Million-Dollar Retirement Plan

Saving $1 million doesn't necessarily mean that you will be able to afford a lavish lifestyle. When drawn down over a thirty-year retirement, $1 million will provide you with a comfortable retirement in many parts of the country, but not an especially extravagant one. If you withdraw 4 percent of a $1 million nest egg each year, you will receive about $40,000 annually before adjusting for inflation. To that amount you can add any Social Security income for which you are eligible. However, if your $1 million is stashed in tax-deferred 401(k)s and IRAs, you will also need to subtract income taxes from that annual income.

Consider an Immediate Annuity

You could use a portion of your retirement savings to purchase an immediate annuity from an insurance company. This is a financial product that will provide you with set payments for the rest of your life, no matter how long you live. An annuity protects you from the risks of outliving your money as well as from stock market downturns. Knowing that you will have enough cash coming in from Social Security and an immediate annuity to cover all of your bills for housing, utilities, and food can relieve a lot of retirement anxiety.

For example, a couple who saved $191,000 could use half of that amount ($95,000) to purchase an inflation-indexed immediate annuity that would provide them with $355 per month and annual increases for inflation until the death of the last surviving spouse. This immediate annuity would provide the couple with a slightly higher annual income than the 4 percent draw-down strategy, while also protecting them from the risks of outliving their money, investment losses, and inflation, according to Government Accountability Office calculations.

However, annuities are insurance products that also have risks. Some annuities charge steep fees, and the mechanics can be complicated. There's also a possibility that the insurance company could go out of business and default on its obligation to make annuity payments. It's important not to put all of your savings into an annuity product, so you will still have money to cope with emergencies. And the money you use to purchase an annuity typically can't be passed on to your children or grandchildren, even if you die shortly after purchasing the product. However, you can avoid this problem by purchasing an annuity that covers the life of both the husband and wife or a product that guarantees payments for a set number of years, even if the account owner dies.

A charitable gift annuity allows you to support the mission of your favorite nonprofit organization, while also improving your retirement finances. When you purchase a charitable gift annuity you hand over a lump sum of cash to a charity and get a tax break plus a steady stream of fixed payments throughout retirement. The amount you give to the charity is an irrevocable gift, and the promised payments to you are backed by the charity's assets. These annuity payments continue throughout the life of the donor no matter how the charity's investments perform. When you die, the charity keeps whatever cash is left. Organizations offering charitable gift annuities include colleges and universities, environmental groups, and social service agencies.

For example, the Consumer Reports Charitable Gift Annuity requires a contribution of at least $10,000 in cash or appreciated securities. It pays one or two annuitants who are age sixty or older a fixed payment for the rest of their lives. Purchasing a charitable gift annuity will also qualify you for an income-tax charitable deduction, and the annuity payments will be partially tax-free. If you purchased a Consumer Reports Charitable Gift Annuity for $10,000 at age sixty, you would receive payments of $440 per year at current rates. This donation would qualify you for a charitable deduction of $2,582.

In addition, $308 of your payment would be tax-free, while $132 would be taxed as ordinary income.

Keep Up with Inflation

Your retirement savings needs to be able to pay for your retirement needs, even as your expenses rise over time. It's important to choose at least some investments that are likely to keep pace with rising costs. Social Security beneficiaries get annual inflation increases each January. Some types of annuity products increase payments to keep up with inflation. Also, the amount of money you invest in Treasury Inflation-Protected Securities (TIPS) increases with inflation and decreases with deflation, in addition to providing twice-yearly interest payments. You can create a ladder of TIPS that mature at different dates to give yourself an additional inflation-adjusted source of income in retirement.

Maintain Your Emergency Fund

The need for an emergency fund doesn't end at retirement. It's important to have some money set aside to cover unexpected expenses so you don't disrupt your draw-down strategy and trigger extra taxes while covering an unexpected expense. A conservative approach is to keep several years worth of living expenses in an FDIC-insured savings account or certificate of deposit. This will give your assets time to recover from any stock market dips so you won't need to withdraw from them while they are down. Using this fund for repairs and emergencies can help you stick to your retirement spending plan.

Managing Risks in Retirement

One of the most difficult aspects of retirement planning is that you don't know how long you will live. If you live longer than you expect to, you risk spending down your savings too quickly. Social Security and immediate annuities both help you manage longevity risks because the payments continue for the rest of your life, no matter how long you live. Withdrawing no more than 3–4 percent of your portfolio each year can also help make sure that your savings will last for the duration of your retirement.

Many retirees choose to shift their money into more conservative assets in retirement in an effort to prevent losses. However, there's also the risk of investing too conservatively. You are likely to be retired for several decades, and will need continued growth in your portfolio during that time to help your savings keep up with inflation. Most people continue to need a diversified portfolio. Social Security benefits are adjusted to keep pace with increases in the Consumer Price Index, which means your payments are likely to keep up with rising costs. Maximizing your initial Social Security benefit will increase the dollar value of your inflation adjustments. Investing some money in Treasury Inflation-Protected Securities, which are also guaranteed by the government to increase in value with inflation, will give you another way to make sure your savings keeps pace with price increases over time.

As you age it's increasingly likely that you or your spouse will develop a health problem or disability. Medicare, especially when supplemented with a Medicare Part D plan and a Medigap policy, will help make your health-care costs more predictable. If you have a low retirement income and few assets, you may be able to qualify for Medicaid, which will help pay for long-term care. However, if you have a moderate income or retirement assets, you can purchase a long-term care insurance policy that will help pay for nursing home costs.

Unplanned Retirement

Retirement is something you try to plan, but sometimes a layoff or health problem can force you into retirement. While you are still working, develop a succession plan in case you need to suddenly retire. It's a good idea to keep learning new skills and to be open to new opportunities in case you should suddenly find yourself back in the job market.

Four Retirement Account Taxes to Avoid

Once you deposit money in a retirement account, aiming to leave it there until your sixties is typically the best way to avoid tax penalties. But you also need to begin taking required withdrawals in your seventies to avoid another, much bigger tax penalty. Correctly timing your retirement account withdrawals could save you a significant amount on income taxes.

1. **Early withdrawal penalty.** There's a 10 percent early withdrawal penalty if you take money out of your traditional 401(k) and IRA before age fifty-nine-and-a-half.
2. **Penalty for failing to take required minimum distributions.** Distributions from traditional 401(k)s and IRAs are required after age seventy-and-a-half. The penalty for failing to withdraw the correct amount is 50 percent of the amount that should have been withdrawn.
3. **Large retirement account withdrawal.** Withdrawing a large amount from a traditional 401(k) or traditional IRA in a single year can result in an abnormally high tax bill. Depending on how close your income is to a higher tax bracket, it could be beneficial to space out smaller withdrawals over several years.
4. **Roth withdrawals from accounts less than five years old.** Roth 401(k) and Roth IRA withdrawals can be tax-free for retirees who are over age fifty-nine-and-a-half, but if your account isn't at least five years old, you might have to pay tax on part of the distribution.

Minimize Social Security Taxes

Up to half of your Social Security benefit will be taxable if the sum of your adjusted gross income, nontaxable interest, and half of your Social Security benefit exceeds $25,000 for individuals and $32,000 for couples. If the sum of these sources of income tops $34,000 for individuals and $44,000 for couples, up to 85 percent of your Social Security payments could be taxable. These income thresholds are not adjusted for inflation, so more retirees will pay income tax on part of their Social Security benefit over time.

Income received from dividends, interest, taxable pension payments, and withdrawals from traditional 401(k)s and IRAs could also lead to your Social Security benefit becoming taxable. Even tax-exempt interest earned on U.S.

savings bonds or municipal bonds counts as income in the equation that determines whether your Social Security payments are taxable. However, withdrawals from Roth 401(k)s and Roth IRAs are not a taxable event and will not contribute to the taxation of your Social Security benefits.

Another strategy that could help you to minimize Social Security taxes is to withdraw money from your traditional 401(k) and IRA accounts before signing up for Social Security. This will get you higher Social Security payments due to signing up at an older age, and lower or no taxes on the benefit payments because the 401(k) and IRA distributions will not be counted as income in a year when you are receiving benefit payments.

You can have your Social Security taxes withheld from your benefit payments. IRS form W-4V allows you to have 7, 10, 15, or 25 percent of your benefit withheld for taxes. If you don't have the tax payments withheld you will need to make quarterly estimated tax payments.

Consider State Taxes

If you will owe a significant amount of taxes on your retirement income, you might be able to reduce the taxes you owe by moving to a state with a low or even no income tax. Seven states do not have an individual income tax: Alaska, Florida, Nevada, South Dakota, Texas, Washington, and Wyoming. The states of New Hampshire and Tennessee tax dividend and interest income only. However, states without an income tax need to get revenue from somewhere else, perhaps through an unusually high sales or property tax.

Downsizing to a smaller home or less expensive neighborhood could reduce your tax bill, as could renting. Some states and local jurisdictions offer property tax exemptions, credits, or rebates to older homeowners who are above a certain age or below a certain income level.

Most states don't tax Social Security or pension income, but a few do. In states that tax retirement benefits, there may be exemptions for people above a certain age or whose adjusted gross income is below a certain amount.

STEP TAKEAWAYS

- If you save in a traditional retirement account, you qualify for a significant tax break during your working years. However, a Roth account allows you to pay taxes up front, so you won't owe tax at all in retirement.

- Watch out for tax penalties if you take money out of traditional retirement accounts before age fifty-nine-and-a-half or fail to take annual distributions after age seventy-and-a-half.

- Part of your Social Security benefit will become subject to income tax if your adjusted gross income and half of your Social Security benefit totals more than $25,000 for individuals and $32,000 for couples.

- You can reduce your tax bill if you hold investments with high tax rates, including Treasury Inflation-Protected Securities and bonds, in retirement accounts while keeping securities with preferential tax treatment, such as municipal bonds and funds that generate long-term capital gains, in taxable investment accounts.

- While it's tempting to move to a state without an income tax, remember to factor property and sales tax into your calculations before relocating in search of lower taxes.

STEP 7

CUT COSTS AND FEES ON YOUR RETIREMENT INVESTMENTS

Fees are one of the biggest destroyers of your retirement savings, especially when compounded over the course of your career. However, it's likely that many of the investment costs you are paying are avoidable. It's a good idea to shop around for the lowest-cost fund that meets your investment needs. In some cases you can get lower fees by maintaining a minimum balance or even just asking.

Even a 1 percent fee can have a devastating impact on your retirement savings over your career or in retirement. If you put $25,000 in a 401(k) account and it earns 7 percent annual returns and is charged expenses of 0.5 percent each year, your account balance will grow to $227,000 over thirty-five years without any additional contributions. However, if you are instead charged 1.5 percent worth of annual fees, your account balance will only grow to $163,000, $64,000 less than you would have had for retirement if you paid lower fees on your investments. In this case, the 1 percent increase in fees reduced your retirement account balance by 28 percent. The fees additionally cause you to miss out on the investment growth the $64,000 would have generated if the money had been left in the account to accumulate.

You can't control how your investments will perform, but you can control how much you pay to own them. Selecting low-cost investment products is one of the most powerful ways to grow your savings faster and retire with more wealth. Here is how to reduce the costs you pay to invest for retirement.

Choose Funds with Low Expense Ratios

The Labor Department requires 401(k) plan sponsors to provide fee information about each investment option to plan participants. You can also find this information in the prospectus for the mutual fund in which the plan invests. Compare several different funds in each investment class you want to own. If one fund charges a much higher fee than another, try to find out what extra value you are getting for the higher cost. If you can't discern a reason for the higher expense ratio, you're better off going with the lower-cost fund.

The typical expense ratio varies depending on the type of investment you are selecting, but as a general rule, an investment that charges more than 1 percent annually is likely to be price-gouging you. It's even better if you can choose funds that charge less than half a percent annually. Sometimes you can find funds that charge less than a tenth of a percent.

You may also be able to negotiate lower costs on your investments. Some financial institutions offer lower expense ratios and reduce or waive fees for people who maintain a certain account balance at the firm or abide by other rules. It's worth calling your plan sponsor to see if there is anything you can do to reduce the fees on your account.

Minimize Transaction Fees

Making changes to your investments can be expensive. Funds often charge transaction fees each time you buy and sell them. Sometimes taxes are also triggered when you make changes. You might be asked to pay a purchase fee when you first buy shares, an exchange fee if you transfer your money to another fund, and a redemption fee when you redeem your shares. Here's a look at some of the fees you could face each time you make changes to your portfolio:

- **Purchase Fee.** This fee is charged when you purchase a fund and is used to pay the fund's costs associated with the purchase.
- **Exchange Fee.** If you exchange your shares in one fund for shares in a different fund within the same group, you could trigger an exchange fee.
- **Redemption Fee.** When you redeem your shares you could be charged a redemption fee. This fee is typically a percentage of the redemption price. The U.S. Securities and Exchange Commission limits redemption fees to 2 percent.
- **Account Fee.** This fee is used to cover account maintenance costs. Some funds change an account maintenance fee to accounts with small balances of less than a certain amount, such as $10,000.

Choose No-Load Mutual Funds

Some mutual funds charge a sales load, which is a fee similar to a commission that could be charged when you first purchase the fund or if you sell the fund within a specific time frame. A front-end sales load reduces the amount invested in the funds you purchase. For example, if you invest $10,000 in a fund with a 5 percent front-end sales load, a $500 sales load will be paid to the selling broker, and if there are no other front-end fees, the remaining $9,500 is invested in the fund. Loads can also be charged on the back end and deducted from your investment earnings when you sell your shares. The fee for a back-end load may change based on how long you hold the investment. You can avoid load fees if you take care to choose no-load mutual funds, but no-load funds could still charge other fees.

Avoid 12b-1 Fees

These ongoing fees are paid out of fund assets. They may be used to pay commissions to brokers or salespeople or to advertise the fund to potential investors. A fund that advertises itself as a no-load mutual fund might still charge 12b-1 fees.

Watch Out for Administrative Costs

There are a variety of expenses involved with setting up and operating a 401(k) plan, including recordkeeping, accounting, and legal services. Some employers pay the 401(k) plan administrative costs on behalf of employees, but others subtract the expenses from employee accounts. There may be an account maintenance fee for each participant enrolled in the plan. Some employers also hire consultants to design or improve the plan or pay for professionals to give investment advice and online guidance, and these costs may also be passed along to 401(k) participants.

Avoid Actively Managed Funds

Funds that are actively managed have an investment manager who takes action to monitor and trade the holdings of the fund in an effort to get a higher return. Management fees are typically charged as a percentage of the assets invested in the fund. Actively managed funds generally have high fees that reflect compensation paid to the fund manager, sales charges, and transaction fees. However, higher investment management fees do not necessarily lead to better performance. The fund manager might not achieve higher returns than the stock market overall, especially once all the extra fees are factored in. While some fund managers may be able to beat the overall stock market returns for a year or two, very few are able to successfully predict the markets over the long term.

Choose Low-Cost Index Funds

Passively managed funds such as index funds aim to track and duplicate the investment returns of an established market index, such as the Standard and Poor's 500. Re-creating an index requires little research or trading, so the costs to own these funds can be very low for investors. Owing an index fund is often a diversified investment in the overall stock or bond market, and your wealth grows at the same rate as the market growth.

Find a Fiduciary

If you use an investment adviser to help manage your portfolio, you will need to pay for that service. Find out how your financial adviser is paid and whether his or her compensation changes based on the investments you select. Some advisers have a financial incentive to recommend the products and services that will make them the most money, even if those investments won't necessarily produce the best possible outcome for you. For example, a broker who buys or sells a stock for you typically charges you a commission. The broker could sell you securities at a marked-up price that is higher than the market price or buy back a fund from you at a below-market rate called the markdown.

Some financial advisers charge an annual fee that is a percentage of your portfolio, while others charge an hourly rate based on the time they spend working for you. A fee-only financial planner who charges a flat fee or hourly rate has no incentive to recommend high-cost funds because his or her compensation does not change based on the investments you select. The Department of Labor recommends asking potential investment advisers if they are willing to act as a fiduciary, which means they will be required to recommend investments that are in your best interest, not their own. Not all people who call themselves investment advisers, wealth managers, financial consultants, or a variety of other impressive-sounding titles have a fiduciary responsibility to work in your best interest. Make sure you choose an investment adviser who is willing to select the investments that are best for your situation, not necessarily the ones that make the biggest profit for the adviser.

Avoid Chasing Returns

Plenty of people rush to buy the latest hot stock, but individual stocks have a vastly greater risk than owning a fund that contains a variety of equities. If you invest a significant portion of your portfolio in a single stock and it declines in value, it could be devastating for your portfolio.

The risk is even greater when you own stocks of the company you work for. If your company goes out of business, you would not only lose your job, but all of your savings that was tied up in the company stock.

FOR EXAMPLE

David, forty-five, is changing jobs. He has $5,000 in his 401(k), but his former employer won't let him keep a balance that small in the old plan and his new employer doesn't accept rollover contributions. He has two options: He can roll the money over to an IRA or cash out the account.

During his job transition, David will have an unusually long gap between paychecks and could certainly use this extra cash. However, taking the cash will trigger a variety of taxes and penalties. Twenty percent (in this case, $1,000) will be withheld for income tax, so the check he receives will only be worth $4,000. Since he is under age fifty-nine-and-a-half, this early distribution will trigger a 10 percent early withdrawal penalty of $500. David's new job puts him in the 25 percent tax bracket for the year, so he will owe another 5 percent in taxes on the distribution, or $250. On his $5,000 401(k) distribution, David ends up having to pay $1,750 worth of taxes and penalties. He only gets to spend $3,250.

Alternatively, David could roll his 401(k) balance over to an IRA account. If he transfers the balance directly from the 401(k) account to the trustee of the IRA account, it won't trigger any penalties, and no portion of his account balance will be withheld for taxes. Income tax will not be due on his IRA balance until he withdraws the money from the account.

Don't try to time the market. While it can be exciting to jump in and out of various funds or choose to invest with the latest hot fund manager everyone is talking about, it isn't likely to improve your returns over the long term. Some people get a rush from trying to buy a fund that will jump in value. Engaging in this type of investing can provide you with plenty of excitement and entertainment. Just don't use money that you can't afford to lose. The fees and tax consequences of changing funds are likely to cancel out many of the gains from going with a hot fund. And almost no funds stay hot indefinitely, which means you could lose money on the transaction.

Before investing in a fund, it's important to take a look at the prospectus. The prospectus will give you a wealth of information about the fund, including its many forms of costs. The expense ratio and other types of transaction fees must be listed in the prospectus. Various fees are identified in a fee table in the fund's prospectus. These tables can be used to compare costs among similar types of funds.

Take Advantage of 401(k) Fee Disclosures

Your 401(k) plan is required to send you a fee disclosure statement each year that provides specific information about the costs of investing in each fund offered by the plan. This document lists the expense ratio as a percentage of the account balance and gives it a dollar value for each $1,000 you invest in the fund. So, if a fund has an expense ratio of 1.04 percent, this document specifies that the fund will cost you $10.40 for each $1,000 you invest in the fund. This allows you to easily calculate that a $10,000 investment in this fund would cost you $104 per year to own. This fee will be deducted from your investment returns regardless of how the investment performs.

Your 401(k) fee disclosure statement will also explain any shareholder fees or restrictions on the fund, and what the charge will be if you take specific actions. For example, there could be a penalty if you withdraw money from the fund before a certain amount of time has passed, or a fee if you need to take an early withdrawal or loan from the account. Hold on to your fee disclosure statement and refer to it each time you need to make a decision about your 401(k) plan.

FOR EXAMPLE

Mary is making an effort to be better informed about her 401(k) plan this year. When her 401(k) fee disclosure statement came in the mail, she decided to read it carefully, rather than tossing it in the filing cabinet with the rest of her statements.

Mary has $50,000 in savings in an actively managed equity fund that has an expense ratio of 1.2 percent. The fund manager claims that he is able to outperform relevant benchmarks and similar types of funds due to his unique skills, but this hasn't consistently happened. Mary is able to see on her fee disclosure statement that the fund has performed about average for an equity fund, which doesn't really justify the high costs. The 1.2 percent expense ratio is costing her $600 per year to own.

Mary decides to switch to a lower-cost index fund. This fund achieved similar returns over the past five years but doesn't have a fund manager and simply tracks the relevant benchmark. This allows the fund to have an especially low expense ratio of 0.05 percent. This fund costs her only $25 per year to own, saving her $575 per year.

Ask for Better 401(k) Options

Some 401(k) plans are filled with hidden costs and high-fee investments. Employees who want to get a 401(k) match and a retirement savings tax break have no choice but to participate in the plan, but some 401(k) plans have such high costs that many of these benefits can be negated. If your 401(k) doesn't offer any investments with reasonable expense ratios, it's worth politely asking your employer to consider adding better options. Instead of harshly criticizing the 401(k) plan, it's more useful to come to the conversation prepared with some potential alternative funds and some talking points about how they will save money for the 401(k) plan and for the employees. Remember that in many cases the human resources representative at your company is likely to be saving in the same 401(k) plan and shares the same interest as you in making the plan better. If you work for a large company with a lot of people who invest in the 401(k) plan, the company may be able to negotiate institutionally priced investments that often have lower fees. Smaller 401(k) plans have less bargaining power and often have retail-priced investments that typically have higher fees.

Remember that no investments are free. Some people think that the investments they own or the financial adviser they use is free because they don't get a bill for these services or see the fees on their account statement. In fact, no fund is free, and financial advisers are professionals who are paid for their time. If you don't know how your financial adviser is compensated and how much you are paying to own a fund, it is your job to find out.

Cutting Costs Is Worth the Effort

A 1 percent fee doesn't sound like a lot of money. A fund charging a 1 percent fee costs you $10 for each $1,000 you invest in the fund. But you can certainly find a better deal. A fund with a 0.5 percent expense ratio would only cost you $5 for every $1,000 invested. And if you shop around for an ultra-low-cost index fund with an expense ratio of 0.05 percent, you could pay just 50 cents for each $1,000 invested.

Choosing a lower-cost fund can add tens of thousands of dollars to your nest egg over the course of your career and throughout your retirement. If you invest $100,000 in a portfolio that charges 1 percent annually in fees, it will cost you nearly $28,000 over twenty years, according to Securities and Exchange Commission calculations. If that $28,000 had stayed in your account, your investments would have earned another $12,000. Without that 1 percent fee deducted, the $100,000 initial investment would have compounded to almost $220,000, assuming the account earned a conservative 4 percent annual return. But the fee and lost investment growth robs you of about

$40,000 over twenty years, leaving you with a final account balance of just $180,000.

While it takes a little effort to seek out a fund with low costs, the payoff over time can be huge. Once you set up a low-cost retirement account, you can let automatic deposits and compounding investment returns take care of the rest of the work for you.

STEP TAKEAWAYS

- Aim to keep your expense ratios under 1 percent, and preferably less than half a percent, to help your savings grow faster.

- Making changes to your investments typically triggers taxes and penalties, so buying and holding will save you money.

- When working with investment advisers, seek a fiduciary, which is someone who is required to recommend investments that are in your best interest, not his or her own.

- Make every effort to minimize the costs associated with your investments. Finding a low-cost fund can save you tens of thousands of dollars in the long run.

STEP 8

CONTROL YOUR HOUSING COSTS

Housing is likely to be your biggest expense throughout your lifetime. Retirement offers you unique opportunities to reduce your housing costs. Your home can be used to reduce your retirement spending and even give your nest egg a quick and significant boost. You can often greatly improve your retirement finances if you are willing to pay off your mortgage, downsize your home, or move to a place with a lower cost of living.

Pay Off Your Mortgage

Paying off your mortgage is one of the best ways to improve your retirement finances. Owning a paid-off house eliminates one of your biggest monthly expenses, because you will no longer need to make mortgage payments or pay rent. You will be able to live comfortably on a much smaller budget once you own your home mortgage-free. To pay off your mortgage faster, you can start making extra payments or put tax refunds or other windfalls toward paying off the balance of the loan. However, once the mortgage is paid off you will still need to pay for other housing costs including property taxes, maintenance, and insurance.

FOR EXAMPLE

Steve and Sandra both worked for thirty-five years and now receive Social Security payments of $2,000 per month. They also have a modest nest egg of $200,000, from which they withdraw another $650 per month. Steve and Sandra's home in Bangor, Maine, costs them $1,035 per month in mortgage payments and other housing expenses. If they continued to pay that housing cost in retirement, it would consume more than half of their Social Security payments every month, leaving them little flexibility to deal with other expenses.

Fortunately, Steve and Sandra made diligent payments and eliminated their mortgage shortly before retirement. While they still have some home-ownership expenses, including insurance, property tax, and maintenance, their monthly housing costs have dropped to $431. Paying off their mortgage is saving Steve and Sandra $604 per month. Now their housing costs only account for 22 percent of their Social Security payments. This allows the couple to more easily afford food, clothing, utilities, and their other retirement expenses. It also leaves a little bit left over for travel and gifts for their grandchildren, things they wouldn't have been able to do with the higher housing costs.

The Joys of Downsizing

If you can't pay off your mortgage, there are other options open to you. One of the most popular is selling your current home and moving into a less expensive house. This can drastically reduce your monthly expenses and perhaps even add to your retirement savings. Moving costs money, so you need to make sure any relocation will generate enough savings to be worth the transaction costs. For example, if you sell your current home for $250,000, move into a house that costs $150,000, and pay $25,000 for moving costs, you could add about $75,000 to your retirement savings.

You're also likely to reduce your taxes, insurance, upkeep, and utility bills from $8,125 at the more expensive house to $4,875 after you downsize, according to calculations by the Center for Retirement Research at Boston College. If you draw down the $75,000 slowly by withdrawing 4 percent each year, you will increase your income by $3,000 per year in retirement. In addition, the smaller bills for the remaining housing expenses save you another $3,250. In this case, downsizing would improve your retirement budget by $6,250 annually. Downsizing to a smaller but newer home could help reduce the time and inconvenience of taking care of a larger and older home.

Consider Relocation

Moving to a smaller, less expensive house will shrink your housing costs; moving to a less expensive state or city will further lower them. Employees often live in high-cost areas to be near their jobs and shorten their commutes. Many parents are willing to pay for expensive housing so their children can go to high-performing public schools. As a retiree, you don't need to pay for costly housing in order to get those types of amenities. You can choose to live in any place that offers the weather, entertainment options, or medical care that suits you best.

Exiting a high-cost city like New York or San Francisco can dramatically improve your retirement finances. In the San Francisco metro area the median home value is $579,300, and it's not uncommon for modest homes to be worth over $1 million. If you are willing to leave the Golden State behind, you can relocate to a place with much more modest housing prices, such as Asheville, North Carolina, where the median home costs $182,100, or Yuma, Arizona, where $118,000 is the median home value.

But a cross-country move isn't always necessary to realize significant savings. Sometimes you can reduce your housing costs by moving across town or within your state. While the median home price for the New York City metro area is $406,700, heading about two-and-a-half hours north to Albany, New York, cuts the median home value in half, to $197,500.

FOR EXAMPLE

Rose and Ronald own a home worth $350,000 in Chicago, Illinois. They moved to Chicago fifteen years ago when Ronald's company offered him a promotion to relocate there, and they purchased their home to minimize his commute. The couple has friends and a social life in Chicago, but their children have moved away for jobs in other cities. Now that they are retired, Rose and Ronald no longer need to live in an expensive home that is close to work, and they wouldn't mind escaping Chicago's traffic and punishing winters. Rose would like to live in a place with enough space for a garden, and Ronald is interested in retiring in a college town where he can take some history courses.

They find a somewhat bigger house than what they have now for $150,000 in Athens, Georgia. After selling their Chicago home for $350,000 and paying $30,000 in transaction and relocation costs, the move enables them to add $170,000 to their retirement savings. The couple is also able to pursue their interests with minimal additional costs. The new house in Athens has plenty of yard space for a garden, and Georgia residents age sixty-two and older are eligible to enroll in college classes tuition-free at the University of Georgia in Athens.

Reverse Mortgages, Renting, and Other Solutions

If you're committed to staying in your current home, you could look into the possibility of obtaining a reverse mortgage. This approach allows retirees age sixty-two and older to use their home equity to pay for retirement expenses. This type of home loan only needs to be repaid if you sell the home, move, or die. A reverse mortgage can be set up as a lump sum, line of credit, or monthly payments that last for the rest of your life or for a specified period of time. However, reverse mortgages often have significant costs including origination, insurance, and service fees. The Center for Retirement Research at Boston College estimates that a reverse mortgage for a house worth $250,000 will trigger $8,250 worth of fees. Reverse mortgages require that you live in the house for the rest of your life. If you leave, the loan becomes due. Additionally, after you take out a reverse mortgage, your home can't be left to your children or other heirs unless they repay the loan.

Become a Renter

A home is likely to be one of your most valuable assets. If you sell your home and become a renter you can use the proceeds of the sale to pay for retirement. Renting has several important advantages over owning a home.

- Renters typically don't have to worry about outdoor maintenance of the property, such as landscaping, cutting the grass, or shoveling snow.
- Instead of having to take care of household problems yourself, you can call the landlord to handle emergency repairs and certain home maintenance chores.
- As a renter, you won't be subject to property taxes, although you may have to purchase renters insurance and sometimes taxes are passed along to tenants in their rent payments.
- Renters may be able to live closer to public transportation or in more walkable communities, which can be useful for retirees who can't or no longer want to drive.

However, renters are at risk for having their rent increased, which can be extremely difficult for retirees with a fixed income to cope with. And, of course, as a renter you live in your home at the pleasure of your landlord. You could be asked to leave the building, which necessitates shopping around for a new place to live.

Creating a Multigenerational Household

Combining residences with your children or grandchildren can cut costs for both parties. You can split housing and utility costs and have more people to share the household chores. Grandparents might be able to provide childcare and meal preparations for busy working parents, and children and grandchildren can help with shopping, transportation to doctor's appointments, and eldercare if you need it. However, if you decide to go this route, it's important to develop clear expectations and boundaries before entering into the arrangement. You don't want to end up in a situation where grandparents impose unwanted parenting advice on their adult children, and live-in grandparents feel resentful about being on-call babysitters.

Sharing Housing

Many retirees end up living alone, especially after a spouse passes away. Sharing your living space can reduce your housing costs and provide opportunities to socialize at the same time. Some retirees rent out a room in their home to generate an extra income stream to help pay their bills. And roommates aren't just for young people. You may want to share housing with other retirees for company and to cut costs.

Retiring Abroad

Adventurous retirees might want to consider moving outside of the United States for retirement. In most cases, your Social Security benefits can be paid to you while you're living in another country. The cost of living in many countries is low enough that Social Security income and a small amount of savings will produce a much more comfortable lifestyle than they would in the United States. Some countries, such as Panama and Belize, also offer retiree residency programs with packages of tax breaks and discounts to attract foreign retirees.

Retirement overseas can certainly be challenging, especially if you don't speak a word of the local language and are unfamiliar with the local customs. You might be worried about crime or diseases you are unaccustomed to. Some careful research on your part will enable you to avoid these things. The quality of health care in Europe, Asia, and Latin America tends to be excellent, and it's often far more affordable than in the United States.

There's no question that moving overseas has a variety of challenges. You will need to get a residency visa to live in another country, which is easier to do for some countries than others. Since you won't be able to use Medicare in another country, you will need to purchase a local health insurance policy in the new country where you will live or an international policy that will work in several countries. Since your retirement savings is likely to be in dollars, your spending power in the new country will be subject to the exchange rate at the time you convert money to the local currency. Before buying property in a foreign country, consider renting for the first year to check out the infrastructure and services, select a neighborhood where you might like to live, and see how you fit into the local culture.

Many other cultures follow a more leisurely pace of life than the United States, which can be difficult for some Americans to adjust to. You will need to decide whether you would prefer to live among the locals in a new country, which could require some foreign language skills, or in an expat community with other foreigners. And you may incur additional costs to communicate with or visit friends and family members back home.

Deciding Where to Live

Retirement is one of the few times in life when you can live anywhere you want to. You can pick up and move to a place that better suits your tastes and the lifestyle you want to lead. Also, a move to an area that costs less can improve your retirement finances in a short amount of time. Here are some factors to consider as you pick a place to retire.

Cost of Living

If you move somewhere with lower costs than where you live now you can drastically improve your retirement budget. If you live in a high-cost city, you may be able to find much more affordable housing in another part of the country. However, there are significant costs when you buy and sell a home as well as moving expenses that you need to factor into your relocation calculations.

Transportation

Many retirees eventually reach a time when they can no longer safely drive. When that happens, it's helpful to live in a place with good public transportation options. It's a good idea to get into a routine of using the public transportation system before you actually need it. Some communities have low-cost or even free public transportation available for senior citizens. If you plan to travel in retirement, it's useful to live near an airport or train station.

Taxes

You may be able to reduce your retirement tax bills by moving to a state with lower tax rates than your current locale. Some states don't have an individual income tax, while others don't levy a sales tax. Property tax breaks for senior citizens vary considerably based on where you live. States also differ in their taxation of Social Security and pension income. Remember to take into account all the various taxes you will pay when deciding whether you will save money on taxes in a new retirement spot.

Climate

If you've had it with shoveling snow and defrosting your car, you can certainly relocate to a place with warmer weather in retirement. But what you save on heating bills might be negated by air-conditioning costs in warmer climates. You should make sure you can tolerate or make other arrangements for often sweltering summers before making the move permanent. You may be able to find a happy medium in a place that offers four mild seasons.

Three Tips for a Sunbelt Retirement

It's fun to dream about living in a place without the hassles of snow and frigid temperatures. But make sure you aren't just trading your snow shovel for an air conditioner.

1. Consider Year-Round Weather

While avoiding another punishing winter might be your first priority, get to know what the weather will be like the rest of the year. A pleasant winter can turn into a brutally hot summer that is too humid to enjoy. While not all retirement budgets will allow this, some retirees head south for the coldest winter months and return north for the temperate summers.

2. Reduce Your Housing Costs

Housing often costs less in the Sun Belt states than in the Northeast or on the West Coast. If you can sell your home in a high-cost area and buy a less expensive home in the Sun Belt, you can add the surplus to your retirement savings.

3. Prepare to Start Over

Moving to Florida or Arizona often means leaving behind the community in which you worked and raised a family. It can take a lot of effort to build friendships in a new place. You will also need to find a new doctor, dentist, and people to help you with home maintenance and repairs, which may take some trial and error. It can help to move to an area that has other older residents who also relocated there from out of town and to volunteer or join other groups in your new community.

Picking the Right Spot

When deciding where you want to spend your retirement, there's no need to rush. This decision is going to have a big impact on the rest of your life. The Internet has given you wonderful tools with which to research. Make a list of locations—whether neighborhoods, towns, cities, or countries—and do some digging about the following things.

Amenities

Make sure that any potential retirement spot has the amenities you want to use in retirement. You may want to make sure you will have access to pools, tennis courts, public parks, or beautiful hiking trails. Perhaps you prefer to immerse yourself in urban pleasures like museums, art galleries, professional sports teams, and a wide selection of restaurants. Living near amenities can give you low-cost entertainment options, help you keep in shape, and make your retirement years more enjoyable.

Local Services

If you have lived in your current town for a while, you probably have someone who knows just how to cut your hair, an auto mechanic you can trust, and a doctor familiar with your health history. If you move to a new place in retirement, you will need to invest the time to find services that meet your preferences all over again. Be prepared for some trial and error as you test out services in a new community, and before you move, make sure all these services can be found within easy distance. Living in a rural area offers many quiet pleasures, but if you're twenty miles from the nearest clinic, it can be difficult to get the health care you need.

Proximity to Family and Friends

It can add joy to your life to retire near your children and grandchildren. Family members might include you in social events and prevent you from becoming too lonely in retirement, especially if your spouse passes away. Relatives may be able to give you a ride to the doctor's office or help you with minor household tasks when you become too old to safely do them. If you don't live near relatives you might need to pay someone else to help with small chores. However, relocating near younger relatives can also be problematic if your children are in careers that will require them to move frequently for their jobs. In this case, you will need to be prepared to relocate again if you want to continue to live near them or be comfortable continuing on in the adopted community without them.

If you don't have family or friends in the area to which you're planning to move, you may want to think through the implications of this. It's easy to become isolated once you no longer go to work every day. Unless you make commitments or social plans, there might not be a reason to leave the house at all. If you move to a new place without people you already know nearby, you will have to make an effort to re-create a social circle. It can help to join clubs or sports leagues, visit the local senior center, or volunteer in the community.

Health-Care Options

It is essential for retirees to live in a community that has medical facilities equipped for diagnosing and treating older patients. If you have an ongoing medical condition or know that a specific illness runs in your family, you could retire near medical professionals who specialize in treating it. You should also find a doctor who specializes in geriatric care and is willing to work with you to make the aging process as gentle as possible.

Some of your health-care concerns are also related to the kind of housing you're moving into. It can make your life easier as you age if you live in a single-story house or the ground floor of an apartment building so you won't have to navigate stairs on a daily basis. You probably also want handles in the shower to prevent slipping and other age-friendly housing features that will make it easier to live on your own as long as possible. Simple changes like getting rid of throw rugs and using only cabinets you can reach without a ladder or chair can do a lot to prevent injuries in retirement.

One type of housing well adapted for this sort of thing is a retirement community. There are a variety of types of housing developments specifically for retirees. You can look into age-restricted communities in which almost all residents are retirees. These communities can range from modest and affordable condos to luxury high-rises. Some communities offer a large number of activities and entertainment and may even take care of maintenance and housekeeping in exchange for an often steep buy-in and monthly fees. If you need help with health issues you can choose an assisted living facility, which will provide access to skilled nursing and medical care onsite. Continuing care retirement communities allow you to progress from independent living to assisted living and skilled nursing home care as your needs change. In general, facilities that provide more medical services and amenities are more expensive.

Job Opportunities

If you plan to work during your retirement years, make sure that any potential retirement spot has career opportunities in the field in which you are interested. While an increasing number of jobs can be performed from anywhere in the country, others are best performed in specific locations. Previous work contacts might be able to help you find work if you continue to live near your former job. If you aren't sure what type of work you would like to do or are considering a variety of possibilities, consider the health of the overall economy in potential retirement spots.

Test It Out

If you are planning to move to a new place in retirement, give it a trial run before you make the move there permanent. A two-week vacation isn't long enough to tell if you will be happy living in a new place. Renting in a new locale for the first year can give you a good idea of whether you will like the place over the long term and in all seasons. It also gives you an extended period of time to check out neighborhoods where you would consider buying a house. If the retirement spot isn't a good fit, renting makes it easy to move on.

Retirement Spots to Avoid

Moving to a seemingly desirable location in retirement doesn't always lead to good results, especially if you don't have any friends or family in the area. Here are some signs a place won't meet your needs as you age.

- **Health-care voids.** Don't move so far away from major health-care facilities that you can't conveniently get the care you need. When an emergency occurs, you want to live near specialists who can effectively treat it.
- **Sweltering humidity.** While many people want to escape winter, constant heat and humidity can be just as bad as extreme cold. Look for year-round pleasant temperatures you can cope with.
- **High-crime areas.** You want to spend time on enjoyable hobbies with loved ones, not worry about being robbed or fear for your personal safety. Ultra-low costs are not worth the risk of becoming a crime victim.
- **Car-dependent communities.** Sooner or later you're going to stop using a car. When you can't drive, it helps you remain independent if your community has reliable public transportation or taxi or van services that help older residents get around town.
- **No nearby friends and family.** As discussed previously, your friends and family provide companionship and valuable help

when you need it. It can be difficult to develop a supportive social circle in a new place. There's nothing wrong with having new adventures, but don't isolate yourself in the process.

- **You can't comfortably afford it.** There are no more pay raises in your future, and Social Security payments only increase by small amounts to keep up with inflation. You don't want to spend your retirement years worrying about where your next mortgage or rent payment is going to come from, or even worse, lose your home.

Staying in Your Current Home

While it's fun to dream about moving to a new place in retirement, most retirees stay put. Your family home and the community in which your children grew up probably contain memories tucked into every wall, floorboard, and tree. This may be the place your children said their first words and learned to ride a bike, and where you shared a variety of other special moments that would be difficult to leave behind.

If you're currently part of a community of people who know you and are willing to lend a hand, hold on to that in retirement. The aging process will be much easier if you have friends and neighbors you can reach out to for company and companionship. A social network can also help you solve problems by offering advice about who they hired to make home repairs or mow the lawn.

Aging in Place

If you want to stay in your current home for the duration of your retirement, you might need to make some adjustments to your home. When it gets dangerous to navigate stairs, it's helpful if everything you need to use is on a single story, including the bedroom and laundry facilities. And your bathroom might need updating with features to help prevent slips and falls, such as grab bars, a walk-in bathtub, and nonskid flooring.

Many communities have services to help retirees live independently in their own homes for as long as possible. Find out whether your city has a meal delivery service and a low-cost taxi or van service specifically for seniors. It's easier to locate and test these services before you need them. And check out the entertainment options at your local senior center. While many of these centers continue to offer traditional activities like bingo and bridge, you might be surprised to find more modern options including computer classes and yoga.

You've probably spent years tinkering with your home and garden to get things just the way you like them, and you will need to start that process over in a new place. Better weather and a couple of tax breaks might not be worth leaving your friends and family members behind. It could take years to set up a social network in a new place and find all the services you need, especially without the connections people typically make at work. Sometimes the best retirement spot is the one you already know and love.

STEP TAKEAWAYS

- Selling your home and moving to a place that costs significantly less can give your retirement savings a quick and significant boost.

- Paying off your mortgage eliminates a major bill, and allows you to use your retirement savings for other costs.

- When considering a new community, pay careful attention to such issues as health-care facilities and transportation.

- Before moving to a new location, give it a trial run—perhaps by renting for a year—before you settle in permanently.

- Most people don't move to a new location in retirement; there are many benefits of staying in a community you already know well.

STEP 9

REDUCE YOUR COST OF LIVING

You may be able to retire sooner if you are willing to reduce the amount you spend each month. Cutting expenses before retirement frees up cash to add to your savings. Also, if you become comfortable living that more frugal lifestyle it reduces the amount you need to save for retirement, because a smaller nest egg will be adequate to pay your retirement bills.

For example, if you switch from a $100-per-month cable TV package to a $20-per-month Internet TV and movie service, you will have reduced your entertainment expenses by $960 per year. You could put that $960 in an IRA and claim a tax deduction for doing so. If you decide you like the less expensive Internet TV service better than cable and stick with it over a twenty-year retirement, you could get by with $19,200 less in savings than you would have needed to pay for cable TV service.

You can further reduce your costs when you are able to ditch work-related expenses. Once you retire, you can eliminate commuting costs and expensive work clothes. Around the same time you may also begin to qualify for senior discounts on many everyday expenses.

But it's equally important to budget for new costs in retirement. Once you have free time to fill you might be tempted to take up traveling or expensive new hobbies, which will add new costs to your budget. If you develop any new health conditions, you could quickly rack up medical bills. It's worth taking a look at how to reduce your expenses in retirement as well as prepare for a few new bills.

Expenses You Can Eliminate in Retirement

There are many ways to reduce your monthly costs in retirement. Some of the costs working people incur disappear when you retire, while other expenses can be significantly reduced if you have the time to put in a little effort. Here are some of the declining expenses you can look forward to in retirement:

Your Mortgage

Paying off your mortgage by the time you retire can eliminate what is probably one of your biggest monthly bills. You will need a lot less income to support yourself in retirement with a paid-off house than if you rent or continue to make mortgage payments. However, you will still need to pay taxes, insurance, and maintenance costs on your property.

Work-Related Expenses

The biggest change in your life after you retire, of course, is that you're no longer working. Aside from everything else, this means a considerable change in your budget. You no longer have to spend money on those things that were necessary for your job.

Commuting

Many working Americans incur significant costs to get to work. Whether you had to pay to put gas in your car or train fares to get to the office each day, this expense will completely disappear once you stop working. You will only need to drive for personal errands or because you want to, which means a lot less spending on gas and less wear and tear on your car. Your car insurance bill may even decrease.

You may also be able to switch to public transportation, biking, or walking for some of your local errands. Some public transportation systems give discounts to senior citizens, and many communities have low-cost van or taxi services that provide transportation to senior citizens at very low rates.

However, if your car is more than a decade old and has a lot of miles on it and you plan to continue to use it in retirement, make sure your budget has room for car repairs or even the possibility that you might need a new car. Getting necessary repairs or even trading an old car in for a new one before you retire can help you to avoid using an unexpectedly large portion of your retirement savings for car expenses.

When both spouses work, they often need separate cars to get to their jobs and perform their work functions. After you retire, you may be able to get by with one car, if you're willing to coordinate your activities with your spouse. Getting rid of one of your cars will also allow you to reduce gas, insurance, and maintenance costs.

Office Clothes

Some jobs require professional clothing that can be expensive and require additional costs for tailoring, dry cleaning, and pressing. Office social events that require dresses and shoes can be even more expensive. Retirees can wear whatever they want to. Jeans don't cost nearly as much as suits.

Work-Related Costs

There are fringe costs associated with working such as lunches out with your coworkers and chipping in for group gifts for colleagues. Many office relationships decline once you leave the workforce, so you will be invited to fewer office social events and both give and receive fewer professional gifts.

Convenience Costs

People who work full-time are busy and often need to pay others to do things they don't have time to do themselves. On a night when you work late you may pick up dinner on the way home because you don't have time to cook. Retirees, however, can prepare meals at their leisure, which saves money. When you're working, you might make quick and impulsive purchases because you have a limited amount of time to get your shopping done on a packed weekend. When you're retired, you have time to comparison shop and negotiate to get the best possible value for your money.

Retirement changes how you function around the house. While you may not have the knowledge to take on every home improvement project yourself, you will probably be able to take on some of the household maintenance you outsourced while working. If you hired someone to cut your grass, clean your house, shovel your sidewalk, or otherwise help maintain your home, you might now have time to take on those household maintenance projects. You may even be able to do some basic home repairs.

Peak Season Travel

Employed people often need to cram their travel plans into long weekends and national holidays, which can be the most expensive and crowded times of year to visit prime vacation spots. Parents of school-age children also drive up travel prices when they all travel during the same school breaks. Retirees have the freedom to choose lower-cost midweek travel and the flexibility to take advantage of last-minute deals. You might choose to do your summer traveling in September, which often still has nice weather. The kids are back in school, the parents are back at work, and you get to enjoy your vacation with fewer people and lower prices.

When you're no longer working, your household may have redundant utilities. You probably won't need both a landline telephone and a cell phone. Paying for both an Internet connection and cable

TV is rapidly become unnecessary because you can watch many shows for free or at very low cost over the Internet. You might be paying for a gym or pool membership you seldom use when you would rather be exercising in a different way. Look for services you pay for that you don't use much or don't produce lasting enjoyment.

Be on the Lookout for Discounts

One great perk of getting older is qualifying for senior discounts. If you are above a certain age you can qualify for discounts on hotel rooms, rental cars, museums, restaurants, and movies. While some senior discounts are widely publicized, others are available only to those who know to ask. Local businesses also might be willing to provide a senior discount to repeat customers.

One particularly valuable senior discount is the America the Beautiful Senior Pass, which gives U.S. citizens or permanent residents age sixty-two or over lifetime access to 2,000 federal recreation sites for just $10, or $20 if you apply for it online or via mail. The free admission applies to your entire vehicle at recreation areas that charge by the vehicle and covers up to four adults at parks with per-person fees. It also qualifies you for discounts on other park amenities including guided tours, camping, swimming, and boat launching.

The organization that once was known as the American Association of Retired Persons—now simply called AARP—negotiates discounts on behalf of its members. It costs $16 per year to join AARP, and the membership fee is discounted if you pay for multiple years up front. You can join AARP as early as age fifty, so you can start using the organization's discounts at an earlier age than many other senior discounts. Discounts provided by businesses might require you to reach an older age, such as sixty-two or sixty-five, before you qualify.

FOR EXAMPLE

While some retirees dread admitting their age, Diane is happy to, so long as you will give her at least 10 percent off her purchase. She signed up for an AARP card for $16 at age fifty and loves flashing it at Outback Steakhouse and Denny's to get 15 percent off her meal. Whenever she travels, her AARP card also qualifies her for discounts on hotel rooms and car rentals.

But senior discounts aren't just for luxuries. Diane knows which local grocery stores offer senior discounts once a week or month and adjusts her shopping schedule accordingly. Grocery store senior discounts are seldom widely publicized, so you often have to ask a store manager or other retirees to find out about them.

Diane isn't afraid to ask for a discount. She is a regular customer at a local bakery, and loves to chat with the owner whenever she stops in. She asked him if his shop would begin providing a senior discount, and ever since then she's been getting 10 percent off her weekly loaf of fresh bread.

However, Diane has also noticed that senior discounts aren't always the best available deal. Sometimes a hotel's promotional deal is better than the AARP rate, and she has seen plenty of cases where an online coupon code or newspaper coupon saved her more than her senior discount would have. Diane spends more time shopping than she did while she was working full-time, and she isn't shy about negotiating for a better deal. The discounts allow her to enjoy a few more little luxuries than she could without those savings.

Personal Finance Savings

Retirement is a time to evaluate how you're handling your finances, not just from the point of view of increasing your retirement income, but also to find ways of saving money. As you approach retirement age, you should start thinking about ways to reduce the cost of your investments, debt load, and taxes.

If you never shopped around for low-cost investments earlier in your career, retirement offers an opportunity to weed out expensive funds. Check out the expense ratio on each fund you own and consider moving your money out of high-cost funds (see Step 7). You could be retired for twenty or more years, so you still have plenty of time to benefit from lower costs on your investments. You will have more money available for spending if less is deducted from your accounts for fees.

Taxes, Debt, and Insurance Costs

While you can't completely eliminate taxes from your retirement budget, as discussed in earlier steps, there's a lot you can do to control them. The investments you made in Roth accounts really start to pay off in retirement because you typically won't have to pay tax on the distributions. You can also space out withdrawals from traditional retirement accounts over as many years as possible so that you can pay a smaller tax bill each year. Another tax minimization strategy involves holding investments with low tax rates, such as stocks, mutual funds that generate long-term capital gains, and tax-exempt municipal bonds, outside your retirement accounts, and keeping investments taxed at higher rates inside your retirement accounts.

Paying off all debt before retirement is a sure way to improve your cash flow. As mentioned earlier, paying off your mortgage can eliminate a large chunk of your housing costs. Eliminating credit card debt removes expensive interest payments from your monthly expenses. Aim to pay off car and home equity loans before retirement as well. You need to use your nest egg to pay for your future retirement expenses, not to pay off debts you took on while working. Remember: The more debt you can retire, the greater your disposable income in retirement.

You probably purchased a life insurance policy when you had young children and a spouse who depended on the income you earned at work. Once you retire, you may not have dependents any longer. That makes this a good time to reevaluate whether you continue to need to pay for a life insurance policy.

Another cost you're done with is that of childrearing. It's certainly expensive to raise children. From childcare and preschool to college costs, you're likely to invest a lot in the education of your children. And that's in addition to food, clothing, afterschool activities, and other things children need. However, once your children become independent adults, these costs go away. Your children may even be a help to you in retirement.

New Retirement Costs to Budget For

While many expenses can be eliminated when you retire, you are also likely to spend more money on a few specific things, including travel and health care. If your retirement budget is tight you will need to take care to invest your newfound free time in saving money, rather than spending to keep yourself entertained. Here are some areas where you could face increased costs in retirement, and what you can do to avoid them:

Entertainment

Retirees have eight or more extra hours of free time to fill every day. Your entertainment costs are likely to grow as you find new expenses to fill up that free time. Some hobbies have high start-up and ongoing costs. For example, if you take up biking, it may not be long before you want an expensive road bike and equipment to maintain it.

Sometimes it's possible to make costly hobbies more affordable. For example, many people dream of a retirement filled with playing golf, but golf is an expensive hobby if you play often. Membership at a private golf club often includes a joining fee and required minimum monthly expenditures. Playing at more reasonable resorts or municipal courses costs significantly less, but could still run you more than $100 per round. People who play regularly often invest in clubs, cleats, and other equipment. Sometimes playing at off-peak time slots can save you money, and some retirees who volunteer or work part-time for a golf club get free or low-cost rounds of golf and discounts at the course store as a perk.

It's useful to seek out free or low-cost activities in your community. Senior centers often arrange entertainment for retirees for free or at very reasonable rates. Many colleges and universities allow locals who are above a certain age to enroll in or audit college classes tuition-free. And strolling along your local lake or river or checking books and movies out of a public library often costs nothing at all.

Travel

Many new retirees have a long-standing dream of travel. After years of squeezing vacations into a week or two of allotted time, you suddenly have the opportunity to spend weeks or months exploring a favored destination. You won't have to rush through each tourist site on your checklist and can instead leisurely take in the scene and interact with the locals.

But taking several extended vacations a year is certainly more expensive than the one or two you were able to fit in while working. Staying somewhere for a month costs a lot more than a weeklong stay, especially if you eat out all the time and fail to negotiate a lower rate for long-term accommodations.

If you plan to do a significant amount of traveling in retirement, it's important to budget for that before leaving your job. There are also ways to make long-term travel plans affordable, especially if you have friends and relatives you can stay with in various places or are willing to pursue creative money-saving options such as housing swaps or traveling with other retirees and splitting the costs. Fortunately, travel deals for senior citizens are abundant. Don't forget to ask for senior or AARP discounts for your hotel, car rental, and other travel costs.

Health Care

This is among the most significant cost increase you will face in retirement. As you age, your chances of developing a health condition that requires care increases. You are likely to need to see doctors more often and perhaps start taking medications or receive treatments to cope with illness or age-related declines in health. While Medicare will cover many of the treatments older people need, your copays and coinsurance costs will increase as you receive more health-care treatment. You can make your retirement health-care costs more predictable by purchasing a Medigap supplement to Medicare and a Medicare Part D prescription drug plan, both of which will fill in some of the costs traditional Medicare doesn't cover.

Three Ways to Reduce Health-Care Costs in Retirement

While you can't completely prevent health-care costs in retirement, there is a lot you can do to avoid surprise medical bills. Here is how to make your retirement health-care expenses more manageable:

1. **Avoid gaps in insurance.** Many people continue to work until they qualify for Medicare at age sixty-five. It's important to sign up on time to avoid delays in coverage and premium increases. If you retire before age sixty-five, make sure you find other health insurance during the interim period, such as COBRA continuation coverage, retiree health insurance, or a policy purchased through your state's health insurance exchange.

2. **Supplement Medicare.** Medicare beneficiaries need to pay 20 percent of the cost of most covered services, which can rapidly become a large amount if you have a significant health problem. A Medigap policy will pay for many of the cost-sharing requirements of traditional Medicare in exchange for a much more predictable premium.

3. **Switch Medicare Part D plans.** Medicare Part D prescription drug plans change their premiums, copays, and covered medications annually. Shopping around for a new plan each year allows you to get the best available coverage at the lowest possible price.

Children and Grandchildren

Even though you no longer have the expense of raising your children, you can face different costs to stay in touch with them. When grandchildren arrive on the scene, their chubby cheeks and gentle gurgles are often a magnet for grandparents. You might incur increased travel costs if you desire to visit out-of-town grandchildren more often. Many grandparents like to shower their grandchildren with gifts for birthdays, holidays, and other special occasions. The expenses for gifts and gatherings can become significant if you have a lot of grandchildren or frequently bestow gifts.

It's not only your grandchildren whom you may be seeing more often. Facing the trifecta of student loan debt, unemployment or a low-paying job, and skyrocketing rental prices, your twenty-something children may want to move back home to get out of debt or save some money for the future. Some retirees will be happy to have their children under the same roof again, while others may be burdened by the expense. It helps to set up ground rules: Will adult children pay rent? If so, how much? Will they chip in for food and utilities? Clearly spelling out who is responsible for what chores or responsibilities can save a lot of headaches and tension in the long run.

Emergencies and Inflation

The need for an emergency fund doesn't disappear when you retire. Your house, car, and household appliances are aging and will probably need to be replaced at some point during your retirement. There may also be health emergencies for you, your spouse, or your parents. Your retirement budget needs to have room for the possibility of unexpected financial shocks. It can be helpful to stress-test your retirement budget to see how your finances might be impacted if you incur a large bill. Take a look at how your finances will change if your roof needs a $2,000 repair or you get a $5,000 emergency room bill.

Aside from unexpected emergencies, inflation will gradually erode the purchasing power of your retirement savings. It's important to take steps to help your retirement savings keep up with rising costs. Social Security payments are adjusted for inflation each year. Some types of government bonds are guaranteed to keep up with inflation. The principal amount invested in Treasury Inflation-Protected Securities, discussed in Step 6, increases with inflation, as measured by the Consumer Price Index, and pays interest at a fixed rate twice a year. But the overall value of this investment could decline with deflation. A few other types of investments have historically kept pace with inflation, including stocks, commodities, and real estate, but this is not guaranteed.

Retirees who have spent decades working and saving often had to make sacrifices to save up enough to leave the working world behind.

FOR EXAMPLE

James wants to play golf twice a week in retirement, but he doesn't want to spend his entire nest egg on his golf habit. He knows that membership at a private golf club could cost thousands of dollars and might include a joining fee and required minimum expenditures. Playing at resorts or municipal courses is less expensive, but it isn't exactly cheap. The cost can easily be $100 or more per round. For example, the cost of a weekday tee-time at the public course Streamsong in Florida starts at $115 if you walk and $145 to ride in a golf cart. The price increases at the most desirable times of year. There are additional costs if you use a caddy or other services.

James doesn't want to spend over $200 per week playing golf, so he decides to see if he can get a discount rate if he works part-time for a golf club. He finds a job as a starter, the person who greets golfers before they start a round and provides information about the course. Many starter jobs qualify the employee for free or significantly discounted rounds of golf. In addition, James now spends his hours at work in a beautiful place chatting about the game. After his work is done, he's welcome to play the course at a significant discount.

Predicting Your Life Expectancy

One of the most difficult aspects of retirement planning is that you don't know how long you will live, so you have to estimate how many years of retirement you need to save up for. While most Americans can expect to live into their mid-eighties, there are certainly some who will die sooner and many who will live far beyond the typical life expectancy. One common strategy for retirees enjoying reasonably good health is to estimate that you will live until 100, just in case you do.

Falling Victim to Fraud

We all like to think we're too smart to fall for a sleazy trick or scam. Many seniors receive phone calls from people pretending to be representatives of the Internal Revenue Service, Social Security Administration, Centers for Medicare & Medicaid Services, or even relatives who ask for personal information over the phone. Some scam artists read the obituary pages and then call the deceased family member's relatives to demand money for an outstanding debt. Fraudulent investment advisers may try to talk you into investments that are inappropriate for your situation or have unnecessarily high costs. In general, don't put your money into any investment product that you don't fully understand, and be suspicious of any stranger who contacts you claiming to be able to improve your retirement finances. More often than not you will need to seek out good deals and solid investment advice yourself.

It's notoriously difficult to determine how long a specific individual will live, but we do know how long the typical person lives. A man born on January 1, 1950, has an average life expectancy of 84.6, according to Social Security Administration projections. A woman with the same birthday can expect to live until age 86.8. However, your life expectancy changes over time. Once a man makes it to age seventy, his average life expectancy increases to 85.8 years and the woman's grows to age 87.7. Of course, your current health, lifestyle, and family history also play a role in how long you will live.

STEP TAKEAWAYS

- Consider using some of your newfound free time to save money in retirement by comparison shopping and negotiating lower prices on the products and services you use.

- Consider reevaluating your retirement budget to eliminate work-related expenses such as travel, clothing, and special events.

- Keep an eye open for useful discounts. They can greatly reduce your day-to-day living costs in retirement.

- Don't be tempted to take up unnecessarily expensive hobbies.

- Reducing your cost of living in retirement frees more money for you to pursue your favorite activities.

- Evaluate your personal finances when you retire, including investments, taxes, debt load, and insurance.

- Many of your costs may go up in retirement, including entertainment, travel, and especially health care. Try to budget for these in advance so they don't disrupt your financial planning.

- Remember to factor inflation into your retirement budget.

STEP 10

REINVENT YOUR LIFE

Retirement isn't simply about hitting a number in your bank account. It's the beginning of a new lifestyle that doesn't involve going to work every day.

You get to tell your boss that you just aren't going to come into work any more. While almost no one gets a gold watch these days, at some offices your fellow employees may throw a party for you or take you to lunch. Some colleagues who didn't save enough for retirement may envy you as they face the years of work ahead of them. Then there will come a moment when you shut down your work computer for the last time and walk out of the office, knowing that you will never have to do this again.

Retirement is a beginning. To some people it feels bittersweet to walk away from office friendships. You are likely to lose touch with people you chatted with every day. You won't get included in the office pools or asked to lunch to commiserate about the boss. You won't get invited to work on an exciting new project or told what a valuable member of the team you are. It can be a shock to realize that you weren't vital or necessary to the functioning of the company. They probably will get along just fine without you.

Many people see retirement as a relief and an escape. You don't have to listen to a condescending boss or sit through pointless meetings. You won't rush all the way to work only to have no one notice your efforts. There are no more office politics to navigate or unnecessarily stressful deadlines to meet. You get to leave all the judgment behind to pursue your own fulfillment.

Choosing When to Retire

It can be difficult to know if you are truly ready to retire. Leaving behind the steady paychecks that have sustained you for decades and becoming dependent on your investments and Social Security to pay all your bills can be a difficult leap to take. It helps to run the numbers and identify just how much you can safely spend each year from your nest egg and compare it to your monthly bills.

Of course, this was easier when you could count on your workplace paying a pension. That gave you a specific number you could count on, no matter how long you lived. But you can't rely on pensions any more because so many of them have been frozen and discontinued. Instead, you need to learn to live without them.

The first step is to estimate how much you will spend each year in retirement. Then get an estimate of your Social Security payments at the age you expect to sign up and subtract that from your expenses. The remaining income must come from your savings, ideally by withdrawing 3–4 percent of your nest egg each year or purchasing an immediate annuity that will provide the remaining required income.

If you haven't saved enough to retire comfortably, working a few extra years can significantly improve your retirement finances. Delaying retirement gives you more time to save and earn returns on your investments and reduces the number of years of retirement your savings needs to pay for. Continuing to work will also increase your Social Security benefit if it allows you to sign up for benefits at an older age.

For example, consider a married couple who needs about $46,900 per year in retirement to pay their bills. If both spouses retire at age sixty-two, the couple will receive about $20,100 in Social Security benefits annually and could purchase an annuity that would provide them with annual payments of the remaining $26,800 for $510,800, according to Congressional Budget

Office calculations. If the couple delays their retirement by one year, their annual Social Security benefit will increase to $21,600 and the price for an annuity to cover the remaining $25,300 of required income drops to $465,000. The amount the couple needs to save to purchase an annuity that will cover their retirement expenses further declines as they continue to delay retirement to $298,400 at age sixty-six and $117,700 at age seventy. Each additional year of work packs a triple punch: It increases Social Security payments, reduces the amount of wealth needed at retirement, and gives the couple's existing savings more time to compound.

But you don't necessarily need to work full-time to improve your retirement finances. A part-time job that pays for some of your current expenses will allow you to draw less from your nest egg each year and give your existing savings more time to compound. Even once you have saved enough to retire, continuing to work a little longer can help you to build up some extra financial security.

However, when you retire is not always a choice. Many people unexpectedly retire ahead of schedule. The median age workers expect to retire is sixty-five, according to an annual survey by the Employee Benefit Research Institute. However, the median age at which people actually retire is sixty-two. Many of the retirees in the survey left their jobs earlier than they expected to due to health problems or a disability that prevented them from being able to continue to do their job. Some people left the workforce to help care for a spouse, parent, or other family member. Retiring early while at the same time incurring growing medical bills can begin to drain your retirement savings. Other retirees were forced out of their jobs due to layoffs or downsizing at their company. A buyout or business closure could toss you into retirement years ahead of schedule. Many retirees in these situations have to find creative ways to make ends meet or significantly reduce their retirement lifestyle. There were also a few positive reasons people retired early, but they were less common. Some people who saved and invested diligently were able to retire ahead of schedule and decided they wanted to do something else instead of continuing to work.

FOR EXAMPLE

Nancy, sixty-five, isn't sure if she is ready to retire yet. Between Social Security payments and her 401(k) balance, she will probably have enough money to pay her bills throughout retirement. However, she thinks her finances might be a little stronger if she stays on the job for an additional year. She considers the benefits of remaining on the job one more year.

Nancy is eligible for $1,000 per month if she signs up for Social Security at age sixty-five. If she delays claiming her payments for one additional year, they will climb to $1,080 per month, or $960 more per year throughout the rest of her retirement. She has $300,000 in her 401(k) account, and she expects to withdraw about $1,000 a month from this nest egg to help pay her bills. If Nancy works another year and lives frugally, she thinks she can tuck an extra $12,000 into the account and get an employer contribution worth another $3,000. These contributions would bring her account balance up to $315,000, not even counting any investment returns. This higher 401(k) balance would allow her to safely withdraw $1,050 per month from her savings throughout retirement, improving her cash flow by $50 per month.

If Nancy's $300,000 nest egg remains untouched for a year and earns a 6 percent return, she will add another $18,000 to her retirement savings. This year of investment gains could add another $60 per month to her retirement budget. Of course, there's also the possibility that Nancy's investments could lose money, so this return is not a sure thing.

Working just one additional year allows Nancy to get $80 more from Social Security every month thereafter. She is able to boost her retirement savings by $15,000, which will add $50 per month to her retirement budget. Finally, she gets another year of investment gains that could add another $60 per month to her retirement income. By delaying her retirement for one year, Nancy will get to spend $190 per month more in retirement.

Unexpected Retirement

Retirement can happen when you are making other plans. Almost half (49 percent) of retirees leave the workforce earlier than they expected to, according to an annual survey by the Employee Benefit Research Institute. An unplanned early retirement is most often due to a health problem, caregiving responsibilities, or job loss. Here is why many people retire unexpectedly early:

Health Problem

An illness, injury, or disability that leaves you unable to continue in your current job is the most common reason people retire early. Obviously, the best way to avoid problems that are so severe you need to leave your job is to maintain your health during your working years. Another way to prepare is to look into how you will maintain your health insurance coverage if you are forced to leave your job due to illness. Get an idea of how much COBRA coverage will cost and what your coverage options are through your state's health insurance exchange (*www.healthcare.gov*) if you need to retire before age sixty-five.

Job Loss

Many older workers find themselves forced out of their jobs years before they would like to retire. Layoffs and business closures can push older workers back into the job market, and if those people can't land new positions in a timely manner they realize that they have unintentionally retired. Key to finding a new job, even at an advanced age, is honing your skills through continuing education classes. That way you can never be accused of having obsolete skills, and can keep yourself open to new job opportunities at any age. A current resume with recently acquired skills that highlight your familiarity with computers and social media savvy can help you land a new job. Job loss in the years leading up to retirement can also be an excuse to change careers or downshift to something part-time or lower-paying that you have wanted to try.

While a job at your local wine shop or tackle store might not pay much, it could provide a little income and a connection to an activity you enjoy.

Caregiving Responsibilities

Some people choose to stop working to help care for a spouse, parent, or other relative who has developed a serious health problem. You can compare the costs of hiring a professional caregiver to how much you earn in the workforce to decide whether it makes financial sense to leave your job to help with caregiving. However, some people also feel that they are able to provide more personalized care than a nonrelative could. Unless you have a flexible job, it can be difficult and expensive to balance caregiving responsibilities with a demanding full-time career.

Windfalls

Of course, unexpected retirement can be rosy if you are able to stop working because investment gains, an inheritance, or another windfall improves your finances. However, this situation is rare and you shouldn't count on it.

Alternatives to Traditional Retirement

Retirement doesn't have to be all or nothing. You don't have to make an abrupt switch from a full-time job to a life of leisure. Some people are able to gradually reduce their hours with their current employer, stay on to consult, or take on the occasional project. Retirement also offers the possibility to test out a completely new career or try out self-employment for a few years.

You may be able to gradually decrease your hours at work. Maybe you could cut back to working four and then three days per week or start coming in for half days. A few companies have formal phased retirement programs, but in most cases this type of arrangement is negotiated on an individual basis. Phased retirement helps companies because the most experienced employees stick around for a few extra years to mentor younger employees and consult on projects. Older workers get to continue to earn a reduced paycheck while also gaining an increased amount of leisure time and perhaps fewer responsibilities at work.

Another alternative is consulting. As an experienced professional you may be able to offer your services to your former employer for some consulting assignments. This allows you to continue to work in retirement on a case-by-case basis, but without the restrictions of needing to go into an office every day.

Some people use retirement as an opportunity to switch to a new field. Perhaps you have always wanted to be a teacher or pastry chef but couldn't make the jump due to the demands of raising a family. Retirement can be a time to test out a dream job and make some money while you're doing it. Ideally, you should secure the new position before leaving your existing job. In some cases you might be able to enroll in a retraining program or boot camp that will put you on the fast track to a new type of job in high demand. The retraining program may even help with job placement.

Once you walk away from your job, it can be very difficult to find a new one if you're in your sixties or older. While federal law prohibits employers with twenty or more employees from discriminating against employees and job applicants age forty and older, discrimination happens. It is, unfortunately, difficult to prove.

Don't let fear of not finding a job or age discrimination get in your way when looking for new employment. Older workers often have many attributes that appeal to potential employers, including years of experience and institutional knowledge of the company or field. They usually have a larger network of connections than young people do. However, many employers are concerned that older workers are not as technically adept as their younger counterparts. Aim to refute such stereotypes during the application process by demonstrating your fluency in social media and various computer programs. It may also help to indicate your willingness to take direction from a younger manager. Be careful not to offend a younger manager by referring to his age or comparing her to your children or grandchildren.

Entrepreneurship and Other Alternatives

A lifetime of accumulated experiences can make retirees ideal entrepreneurs. People who have spent a decade or more in a given industry often know what innovations are needed better than anyone else does and have the knowledge and logistical capabilities to pull it off. Some people even start businesses that serve the companies they once worked for. Knowing the people who would benefit from buying your product or service can help get your new business off to a fast start. Having worked in the industry gives you insider knowledge about tailoring your business to be especially useful to clients and customers. Just don't invest retirement money that you can't afford to lose in the business.

Indulge in a Mini Retirement

Some people want to retire because they can no longer tolerate going into a job they dislike. People who are overworked and stressed might need a significant vacation, perhaps three to six months or even a year, to rest and recharge. But after that, they might be ready to launch a second career. Whether you call it a trial retirement or an extended vacation, you can take some time for yourself while leaving yourself open to the possibility of something new.

Of course, just because you've left your old job doesn't mean you have to go back full-time. Depending on your interests, you might choose to work part-time at a golf club, winery, museum, or library. Part-time jobs in a field in which you are interested often offer many social benefits as you interact with coworkers and customers who have similar concerns. For example, working in a wine shop might allow you to chat with customers about the latest varietals and get discounts on bottles you wish to add to your collection. You may get to have flexible hours or work seasonally. Keep in mind, though, that a part-time job may not pay very well, and will seldom come with benefits.

FOR EXAMPLE

Matthew, sixty, doesn't really like his job. While his marketing position pays $75,000 per year, it's stressful and unpleasant, and he doesn't get paid nearly enough for the aggravation he goes through during his long commute. Now that he has finished paying for college for his two children, he would really like to retire.

The problem is that he can't really afford to retire yet. He isn't old enough to sign up for Medicare or Social Security. He does qualify for penalty-free 401(k) and IRA withdrawals, but he only has $100,000 in his retirement accounts and knows he should save that for when he's older and unable to work. His $100,000 nest egg is really only enough to provide just over $300 per month in retirement income, which won't come close to paying his bills. And he needs the health insurance he gets through his job.

Matthew requires income to pay his current bills and help his nest egg continue to grow, but he doesn't necessarily need to earn the same salary he does now. He is also interested in using his marketing skills in a more meaningful way. He ends up taking a marketing job at a nonprofit that helps fund music programs in public schools. The nonprofit job pays much less, just $45,000 per year. However, that's enough to allow him to pay his bills and continue to save a little more for retirement, and it provides much-needed health insurance. Plus, Matthew feels good about the work he is doing.

Coordinating Retirement with Your Spouse

If you're married, you and your spouse have two retirements to plan for. Some couples try to coordinate their retirements so they can enjoy their retirement years together, while others retire years apart. There are benefits and drawbacks to each style of retirement.

Couples who retire together will have time to relax, travel, and have fun. But retiring together is different from spending a week or two together on vacation. After years of only spending evenings and weekends together, it can be disconcerting to be together all day, every day. Your companion can get on your nerves when you are used to having privacy. You will need to decide how much time to spend together and when you will pursue separate interests. This may lead you to develop a new routine that meets both of your needs for attention and alone time.

Some spouses retire years apart by design or circumstance. Especially if there is a big age difference between you, one partner may be ready to retire, while the other is engaged with his or her career. One spouse might be forced into retirement and unable to find a new job. Having at least one of you continue to work can be good for your finances. If you're too young to qualify for Medicare, a working spouse can provide affordable health benefits for both of you. However, if one of you is working and the other isn't, you may need to renegotiate household chores. The working spouse probably expects the nonworking spouse to do more of the housework and meal preparation and will be disappointed if that doesn't happen. The nonworking spouse may want to do more traveling, going out, or entertaining than the spouse who worked all day has the energy for.

Married couples don't always agree on retirement timing or the lifestyle they wish to lead. Some retirees want to constantly travel, while others are happiest spending time at home. One of you might want to retire near the beach, while the other wants to stay in the community where you raised your children. While some people want to spend time with their grandchildren every day after school, others don't want to be free babysitters but would be perfectly fine with the occasional weekend or holiday visit. It's important to talk to your spouse about what you want your retirement to be like.

Deciding How to Fill Your Days

While finding a way to pay for retirement is important, the experience of retirement is about finding meaningful ways to spend your time. You can choose to stretch out your days relaxing or fill your days with hobbies and volunteer work. You might pursue both during different parts of your retirement. While you may enjoy relaxing for the first few weeks or months of retirement after an exhausting career, some day you will want to leave the house, be with other people, and perhaps find a way that you can contribute to the community and help others.

Eventually someone is going to ask you the question, "What do you do?" Most working people answer with their occupation. Retirees need to think of a new answer. Your response can be funny or serious, but don't be unprepared for the question.

How Retirees Spend Their Time

Retirees enjoy significantly more leisure time than their younger counterparts. People over age sixty-five spend the bulk of their newfound free time watching nearly four hours per day of TV, according to the American Time Use Survey by the Bureau of Labor Statistics. People ages sixty-five to seventy-four also spend a significant amount of time sleeping and engaging in other personal care activities (9.4 hours). Other popular leisure activities include house and garden projects (2.45 hours), eating and drinking (1.41 hours), working (1.15 hours), and reading (.74 hours), all of which retirees linger over longer than younger people.

It can help to talk to current retirees about their experiences during this transition. It's possible you'll have so little to do in retirement that you'll become bored. On the other hand, you may sign up for so many activities and projects that you're overwhelmed in retirement, just as you were at work. Ask retirees how they found a happy medium, and what you can do to make the retirement experience more enjoyable.

The transition into retirement is often smoother if you start to set up this new lifestyle before you retire. This is a time in life when you finally get to decide how you want to spend your time, where you want to live, and who you want to be with. It can be useful to test out several retirement options to see what will be the best fit, and to remain flexible and make adjustments as you progress through retirement. Here are some ideas to fill your days in retirement:

Slow Down

Retirees get eight or more extra hours of free time each day. Watching TV is the most popular leisure activity, and retirees spend almost four hours per day in front of a screen. They also spend more time reading and relaxing than their younger counterparts. Retirees don't need to hurry through activities the way many working people do. Retirees spend a few minutes more each day lingering over meals, working on home and garden projects, and shopping. You finally have the time to stop and chat with people as you run your errands and can hang out on your coffee break as long as you want to. Instead of rushing to check off items on your to-do list, you can take things a little slower and do them correctly instead of just quickly.

Take Up a Hobby

Retirement is a time to rediscover interests you didn't have time for while working full-time and raising a family. Some people choose artistic pursuits such as drawing or painting, while others tinker in the garden, brush up on a long-neglected musical instrument, or challenge themselves to pick up a new language.

Get Healthy

Working people sometimes claim they don't have time to exercise. Retirees don't have that excuse. You could take a walk around town after dinner each evening or find a local hiking spot to get some extra exercise. Equally important is staying mentally fit by continuing to engage in cognitively challenging activities. Take your time preparing healthy meals and find a tasty way to prepare the foods you know you should be eating. You can set up your life so that you can avoid stress and the constant need to hurry. If you have any nagging health problems, get to a doctor and set up a professional treatment plan. Without the need to report to work, you can toss out your alarm clock and finally get all the sleep you need. Aim to set up a lifestyle that allows you to be as healthy as you can.

Go Back to School

Taking college courses as a retiree is often much more affordable than it was earlier in your life. Many public colleges and some private institutions offer tuition waivers to students who are above a certain age. Other colleges allow retirees to audit classes for free, but those students do not receive college credit for their coursework. Some higher education institutions also offer classes specifically for retirees. The Osher Lifelong Learning Institute has more than 100 locations on college campuses that provide noncredit classes specifically for older students. And people of any age can take online courses taught by professors from top universities for free. If you truly want to relive the college experience, some colleges have university-affiliated retirement communities on or near campus, and residents often get access to campus amenities, such as the athletic facilities, libraries, and on-campus concerts and performances.

Do Volunteer Work

Working people tend to make their contributions to society through their jobs. Some retirees come to miss the feeling of being useful to others and contributing to a larger goal. Signing up for a volunteer position allows you to contribute to a worthy cause while also being able to socialize with other people who enjoy the same interests. Museums often need docents, your local park or community garden might need someone with gardening skills, and there are nonprofit and charitable groups for almost every cause you can imagine. A volunteer position allows you to help others and add meaning to your retirement years.

Travel

New retirees who had a limited amount of vacation time while they were working often have a pent-up desire to travel. Retirees have the time to explore a destination for an extended period of time, rather than checking off all the major tourist sites in a week. Moreover, you aren't confined to school breaks, national holidays, and long weekends. Instead of traveling during the peak times for a given destination, you can arrive during the shoulder season, when there are smaller crowds and lower rates. Senior discounts for travel costs abound, especially for hotels and rental cars, and many museums and tourist sites also provide discount admission to people above a certain age.

Socialize

Without a job to prompt you to leave the house each day, it's easy to become isolated at home. Make the effort to meet up with old friends for lunch. Invite your neighbors over for dinner. You're no longer obligated to attend social events with people you dislike, but make an effort to set up some social events with those whose company you enjoy. Try to meet some new people in retirement. You may want to find some other retirees who can relate to the perks and challenges of retirement.

Get to Know Your Grandchildren

You may have been too busy working to spend as much time with your children as you would have liked to. You get a second chance when your grandchildren arrive on the scene. If your grandchildren live nearby, you might be able to set up a weekly playdate, plan special outings, or volunteer in their classroom at school.

Become a Penny Pincher

If you have more time than money in retirement, there are a variety of simple strategies you can use to improve your budget. Clipping coupons and waiting for sales when you do your shopping can save you money, especially if you combine these strategies. You can negotiate a lower rate for your cable bill, look for investment products with lower fees than what you have now, and cancel services you no longer need. You may be able to negotiate lower rates on many of your bills. And remember to always ask for a senior discount.

Improve Your Home

You don't need to pay for expensive home improvements when you can take care of some projects yourself. You may be able to refinish an old piece of furniture instead of buying a new one or landscape your yard instead of hiring a gardener. Some people get an incredible amount of satisfaction from beautifying their home with their own hands.

Leave a Legacy

Some retirees aim to leave a financial legacy for their children or a desired institution or charity. In this case you will need to spell out your wishes in a will and make sure all your financial accounts have updated beneficiary forms. You may also want to leave a written or photo legacy. You can write an autobiography, compose letters to your children or grandchildren, or collect and organize family photographs and properly label them. You could get a genetic test to see what's written in your genes, or research your family's genealogy and write up a report for future generations. Retirement can be a time to decide how you want to be remembered.

STEP TAKEAWAYS

- Delaying retirement gives you more time to save for retirement and shortens the number of retirement years you need to pay for.

- You can gradually transition into retirement by cutting back your hours, finding a part-time job, or taking on consulting work.

- You need to decide whether you will retire together with your spouse or have one spouse remain in the workforce.

- Develop a plan for how you will spend your time in retirement.

APPENDIX A
A RETIREMENT PLANNING CHECKLIST

Each type of retirement benefit has important deadlines you need to meet to qualify for benefits or tax breaks and avoid penalties. Pay attention to these deadlines when making retirement planning decisions.

Decide When to Start Social Security

Create a My Social Security account at *www.ssa.gov/myaccount* to verify your taxes paid and get a personalized estimate of the retirement benefits for which you are eligible. You need to decide when you will sign up for Social Security (*www.ssa.gov/retire/apply.html*) between ages sixty-two and seventy. Keep in mind that benefits are reduced for early claiming and increased for later claiming, and that you can coordinate your benefit with your spouse. You do not necessarily need to sign up for benefits in the year you retire.

Sign Up for Medicare on Time

Take care to sign up for Medicare at *www.ssa.gov/medicare/apply.html* during the seven-month window around the month you turn sixty-five to avoid late enrollment penalties. Once enrolled, get your "Welcome to Medicare" exam and any necessary screenings or tests. Develop a treatment plan with your doctor for managing or preventing health problems. You can examine the Medicare Part D options in your area using the Medicare Plan Finder at *www.medicare.gov/find-a-plan* and make changes to your coverage during the open enrollment period from October 15 to December 7.

Finish Funding Your Retirement Accounts

The year before you retire is often your last chance to tuck as much money into retirement accounts as you can. Use your final paychecks to give your nest egg a boost and reduce your tax bill at the same time. You need earned income to participate in an IRA or Roth IRA, so once you and your spouse stop working you can't put any more money into these accounts. 401(k) accounts are connected to your job, so you can no longer make new contributions once you leave the company.

Review Your Plan to Spend Your Savings

Estimate your annual expenses and compare it to the retirement income you will have from Social Security and withdrawing 3–4 percent of your savings each year. You can also add in any other income streams you might have from other sources. If this is enough to cover your retirement expenses and you have a little extra for unexpected expenses, you can feel comfortable that your money is likely to last the rest of your life.

Consider Consolidating Your Retirement Accounts

If you have several different 401(k)s and IRAs, it can simplify your finances to consolidate them into one traditional IRA and one Roth IRA. Fewer accounts make it easier to track and rebalance your investments, and you will have fewer required minimum distributions to calculate. You may even be able to get lower fees on your investments if you maintain a larger balance at a single financial institution.

Remember Required Minimum Distributions

Annual withdrawals from your 401(k), IRA, and Roth 401(k) are required after age seventy-and-a-half. You can delay your first required minimum distribution until April 1 of the year after you turn seventy-and-a-half, but subsequent distributions are due by December 31 each year. There is a 50 percent tax penalty on missed required minimum distributions.

Decide How You Will Spend Your Time

While your finances are an essential part of a successful retirement, there are other important aspects of retirement planning. You need a plan for how you will spend your time so you don't become bored or lonely. While you will certainly want to relax during the first few weeks or months of retirement, after that you may want to start activities that add challenge or meaning to your retirement years.

Important Ages for Retirement Planning

You need to pay attention to your age when making retirement decisions. There are deadlines for claiming various types of retirement benefits and avoiding penalties associated with them. Here are some important age-related benefits to pay attention to:

- **Age fifty.** Workers age fifty and older are eligible to make catch-up contributions to their 401(k) and IRA accounts. Older workers can defer taxes on as much as $24,000 in 401(k) plans and $6,500 in IRAs in 2016, which is $6,000 and $1,000 more, respectively, than the amounts for younger employees.
- **Age fifty-five.** People who lose or leave their jobs in the calendar year they turn age fifty-five or later won't have to pay the early withdrawal penalty on distributions from the 401(k) plan from their most recent job.
- **Age fifty-nine-and-a-half.** There's no longer a 10 percent early withdrawal penalty on 401(k) and IRA distributions after age fifty-nine-and-a-half.
- **Age sixty-two.** You can claim Social Security benefits beginning at age sixty-two, but payments are permanently reduced if you sign up at this age. If you work and collect Social Security benefits at the same time, part or all of your benefit payments could be temporarily withheld.
- **Age sixty-five.** The seven-month initial enrollment period for Medicare begins three months before your sixty-fifth birthday. If you don't sign up on time, your Medicare Part B and D premiums could permanently increase, and you could be denied

the opportunity to purchase supplemental coverage. If you are still working at age sixty-five, you need to sign up within eight months of leaving the job or group health insurance plan to avoid the higher premiums.

- **Age sixty-six.** You can begin to collect the entire Social Security benefit you have earned at your full retirement age, which is sixty-six for baby boomers born between 1943 and 1954. The full retirement age increases from sixty-six and two months for people born in 1955 to sixty-six and ten months for workers born in 1959. At full retirement age and older, Social Security benefits are no longer withheld if you work and collect Social Security benefits simultaneously.
- **Age sixty-seven.** The Social Security full retirement age is sixty-seven for people born in 1960 or later.
- **Age seventy.** Social Security payments further increase by about 8 percent per year for workers who delay claiming them up until age seventy. After age seventy there is no additional benefit for waiting to claim Social Security.
- **Age seventy-and-a-half.** Distributions from traditional IRAs, 401(k)s, and Roth 401(k)s are required after age seventy-and-a-half. Income tax will be due on withdrawals from the traditional retirement accounts, but not the Roth IRA. Employed individuals who don't own 5 percent or more of the company they work for can delay distributions from their current 401(k) until April 1 of the year after they retire. Investors age seventy-and-a-half and older are no longer eligible for a tax deduction on their traditional IRA contributions.

There are also important calendar year deadlines for retirement accounts and Medicare coverage. Make sure you meet the deadlines for contributing to and withdrawing money from retirement accounts and shopping around for new Medicare coverage each year.

December 31

401(k) contributions typically need to be made by the end of the calendar year. Required minimum distributions from retirement accounts (except for the first one) must also be taken by December 31 each year to avoid a 50 percent tax penalty on the amount that should have been withdrawn.

April 1

You can delay your first required minimum distribution from a 401(k) or IRA until April 1 of the year after you turn seventy-and-a-half. However, your second and all subsequent distributions will be due by December 31 annually. So, delaying your first distribution will require you to take two distributions in the same year, which could result in an unusually high tax bill that year.

April 15

You can make IRA contributions until your tax filing deadline, which is typically around April 15 each year. Contributing to an IRA in April can result in nearly immediate tax savings on your current bill.

October 15 to December 7

Medicare Part D beneficiaries have the option to switch plans (do this at *www.medicare.gov/find-a-plan*) between October 15 and December 7 each year during the annual enrollment period. During this time period you should check that the medications you need will continue to be covered at an affordable price. If they will not be, consider switching plans. You can also join a Medicare Advantage plan or switch back to original Medicare. If you swap plans your new coverage will begin on January 1.

Meeting these deadlines is crucial for your retirement planning success. If you don't take action by a specific date or age, you could trigger penalties or fees or miss out on a valuable retirement benefit you could have gotten.

Five Websites Every Retiree Needs to Visit

You can sign up for Social Security and Medicare online, at a time that's convenient for you. There are also several useful websites that can help you make important decisions about the timing and selection of your benefits. You will be able to get the services you need more easily if you familiarize yourself with these websites.

1. Create a My Social Security Account

www.ssa.gov/myaccount. There's no need to wait for a paper Social Security statement in the mail. You can view your Social Security statement online at any time. This important document includes your earnings history, taxes paid, and a personalized estimate of your future Social Security benefit if you sign up at various ages. You can also find out how much you will be eligible for if you become disabled and what your family members might receive if you pass away.

2. Apply for Social Security Benefits

www.ssa.gov/retire/apply.html. There are no lines or wait times when you sign up for Social Security benefits online. You can start and stop your application at your leisure and submit your claim for payments without leaving your house.

3. Apply for Medicare

www.ssa.gov/medicare/apply.html. This website allows you to sign up for Medicare online, while continuing to delay claiming Social Security until later. Applying for benefits from home saves a trip to the Social Security office and makes it easy to gather the paperwork and fill out the application at your convenience.

4. Medicare Plan Finder

www.medicare.gov/find-a-plan. This website provides extensive information about the costs and coverage of every Medicare Part D plan that is available in your area. Retirees with Medicare Part D plans should use the Medicare Plan Finder every year to make sure that their medications will continue to be covered at the best possible price.

5. Health-Care Exchanges

www.healthcare.gov. If you want to retire before you are eligible for Medicare, you should take a look at the health insurance offered through your state's health insurance exchange. Each state offers a variety of coverage options and subsidies to help pay for them if you qualify. These plans are not allowed to reject you or charge you more because of any pre-existing medical conditions.

APPENDIX B
GLOSSARY

401(k)

An employer-sponsored retirement savings account that allows workers to defer paying income tax on their deposits.

401(k) fee disclosure statement

A document 401(k) plan sponsors are required to give plan participants that outlines the costs of each investment option.

Automatic enrollment

A portion of worker paychecks are withheld and deposited in a retirement account without the employee initiating the transaction.

Actively managed fund

A professional fund manager decides which investments to buy and sell within the fund with the goal of superior investment performance.

Default investment

The fund 401(k) participants are automatically invested in unless they choose another fund.

Defined benefit plan

A retirement plan that guarantees a specific payout to workers who meet certain job tenure and age requirements.

Defined contribution plan

An account in which you or your employer are free to decide how much to contribute to the plan and also free to change that amount at any time.

Expense ratio

The annual fee charged to shareholders by funds.

Fiduciary

A professional who is legally or ethically required to work in another person's best interest.

Immediate annuity

An insurance product that provides payments for a set period of time or the lifetime of the purchaser.

Index fund

A collection of stocks or bonds designed to capture the returns of the entire stock or bond market or a specific sector of the market.

Individual retirement account

A retirement investment account in which workers can delay paying income tax on their contributions until the money is withdrawn from the account.

Medicare

The government health insurance program for people age sixty-five and older.

Medicare Part A

Hospital insurance that covers inpatient care at a hospital, hospice care, and some types of home care.

Medicare Part B

Medical insurance that provides coverage for doctor's visits, outpatient care, and some preventive services.

Medicare Part C or Medicare Advantage Plan

An alternative to original Medicare in which Medicare-approved private insurance companies provide hospital, medical, and sometimes prescription drug coverage, often with additional restrictions on coverage.

Medicare Part D

Medicare-approved private prescription drug plans that pay for some of the costs of medications.

Medicare Plan Finder

The website where you can research your Medicare Part D options. *www.medicare.gov/find-a-plan*

Medigap

A supplement to original Medicare that covers some of the out-of-pocket costs of original Medicare and some extra services in exchange for an additional premium.

My Social Security

The website where retirees can view their online Social Security statements. *www.ssa.gov/myaccount*

Reverse mortgage

A home loan that allows retirees to use their home equity to pay for retirement expenses.

Roth 401(k)

An after-tax workplace retirement account that can provide tax-free retirement income.

Roth IRA

An after-tax retirement savings account that provides tax-free investment growth and the potential for tax-free income in retirement.

Saver's credit

A tax credit for low- and moderate-income workers who contribute to retirement accounts.

Social Security

A federal insurance program that provides payments to retirees, survivors, and disabled people who have paid into the system.

Social Security full retirement age

The age at which retirees qualify for the full Social Security payment they have earned. The full retirement age varies by birth year.

Target-date fund

A fund that includes a mix of equities, bonds, and cash that gradually shifts the investment mix to become more conservative over time.

Vesting

Ownership of an asset that cannot be taken away.

APPENDIX C
HOW TO GET A PENSION

A pension plan is a retirement benefit that provides income to former employees. A specific monthly benefit is paid to retirees after they meet job tenure and age requirements.

Pension plans are often referred to as defined benefit plans, because the employer guarantees the amount you will receive in retirement. The formula for calculating retirement payments differs by company. Your salary, years of service, and age are factors commonly used to determine retirement benefits. For example, your pension payouts might be calculated to be worth 1 percent of your average salary for the last five years of employment, multiplied by your years of service.

Your employer and the federal government bear most of the risks of traditional pension plans. The company or union sponsoring the plan typically must fund the pension plan and appropriately invest the accumulated assets. Investment declines or business failures typically do not impact an individual employee's retirement payments because most traditional private-sector pension plans are insured by the federal government up to certain annual limits.

Pension plans, though they have been in decline for a long time, still exist in a handful of specific jobs and industries. Government employees, union members, and employees at a few large companies in specific fields are among the fortunate few who continue to enjoy the financial security of guaranteed payments in retirement.

A Guide to Getting a Pension

A significant minority of private industry workers (18 percent) were provided with a traditional pension plan through their jobs in 2015, according to Bureau of Labor Statistics data. However, a few career fields continue to provide the majority of traditional pension plans. Here's how to get a job that will provide you with a steady stream of payments in retirement.

Get a Government Job

Among state and local government workers, 84 percent had a traditional pension plan in 2015. Primary, secondary, and special education teachers enjoy almost universal (98 percent) traditional pension plan coverage. Members of the protective service (86 percent) and those employed working with natural resources, construction, and maintenance (90 percent) also enjoy strong rates of pension membership. Government workers involved in health care and social assistance (68 percent) or who teach at colleges, junior colleges, and universities (77 percent) have slightly lower rates of pension coverage, although still much higher than in the private sector. Government employees in the Midwest (79 percent) are less likely to have traditional pension plans than public employees in the rest of the country.

Join a Union

A union card just might be your ticket to better retirement benefits. Unions negotiate with company management for better retirement benefits for their members. That's why 72 percent of union members continue to enjoy traditional pension plans, compared to just 13 percent of nonunion employees. Collectively bargaining for better retirement benefits often yields better results than negotiating on your own.

Work for a Big Company

Large employers are much more likely to provide a traditional pension plan than small businesses. Among firms with 500 or more workers, 43 percent have a traditional pension plan. Only 21 percent of employers with between 100 and 499 workers provide a pension, and it drops to 8 percent among companies with fewer than 100 employees.

Join a Very Small Firm

Most small businesses don't provide traditional pension plans to employees, but the exception is ultra-small companies with five or fewer employees. Sometimes small groups of professionals, such as doctors, dentists, or lawyers will set up a pension to defer some of their compensation for retirement.

Move to the Northeast or Midwest

Jobs in the Northeast and Midwest are more likely to provide traditional pension plans than employment opportunities in the West and especially the South. The Middle Atlantic region has the highest rate of traditional pension coverage, with a quarter of private industry workers eligible for a pension. In the East South Central area, just 12 percent of workers have the option to join a pension plan.

Join the Management Track

Managers, especially those who work in business and finance, have better retirement benefits than most other occupations. Some 30 percent of private-sector employees in a management role have a traditional pension plan.

Work Full Time

Many pension plans are closed to part-time workers. While 22 percent of private-sector full-time employees have a pension plan, just 9 percent of their part-time counterparts are eligible to participate.

Earn a Large Income

Over a third (36 percent) of workers in the top 10 percent of the income distribution also have a traditional pension plan. Only 6 percent of people in the bottom quarter of the earnings distribution enjoy the same level of retirement security.

Carefully Consider Your Profession

A few specific industries are especially likely to maintain traditional pension plans. The majority of employees who work for utility companies (78 percent) have pension benefits. Also, just over half (51 percent) of people who work for credit intermediation firms have pension plans.

Other industries with above-average rates of pension coverage include insurance carriers (48 percent), information services (47 percent), transportation and warehousing (34 percent), and manufacturing (27 percent). Leisure and hospitality jobs (3 percent) and especially food service (2 percent) are the least likely to provide retirement benefits.

Stay at the Same Job for Much of Your Career

Working at a firm that provides a traditional pension plan doesn't mean you will get payouts in retirement. You will likely need to work for a specific number of years for the same employer before you qualify. If you change employers, you might not qualify for any retirement payout at all, or only a very modest one. Most pension plans are set up to provide the biggest rewards to people who spend decades with the same employer.

Marry Someone with a Pension

If you are or were married to someone who vested in a traditional pension plan, you may qualify for traditional pension payments, even if your spouse with the pension passed away. Traditional pension plans are required to provide qualified joint and survivor annuities to spouses. However, over a third of married couples with pensions opt not to receive a spousal survivor benefit, often to get higher monthly payments in the short term, according to a GAO report.

Create Your Own Pension

If you have some savings, you can create a stream of retirement payments using an immediate annuity. (See Step 6 for more information on how to do this.) This insurance product provides payments that are guaranteed to last the rest of your life. However, they're also known for fees, complicated mechanics, and the risk that the insurance company could go out of business.

Keep Track of Your Pension

Once you get a job with a pension, make sure you locate and keep copies of documentation that spells out what you will be entitled to. A document called the summary plan description will explain the requirements for earning benefits, how the pension will be calculated, and when you can receive payments. You will also receive individual benefit statements that you should keep in a safe place. Pension plans are required to file paperwork about their funding with the government each year. You can check up on the financial health of your pension plan by requesting a copy of form 5500.

You need to be vested in a pension plan to qualify for payments. The summary plan description typically explains how you become vested in the plan. Some employers have cliff vesting schedules that require as much as five years of service before you will receive any type of retirement payout. Other companies use a graduated vesting schedule in which employees vest in a proportion of the plan based on their years of service, but don't become fully vested until they hit as much as seven years of service. For example, an employee might be 20 percent vested after three years, 40 percent vested after four years, 60 percent vested after five years, 80 percent after six years of service, and fully vested when she or he hits seven years of job tenure. Pension plans calculate retirement payouts in a variety of different ways. Most private-sector pensions do not provide cost-of-living adjustments, but a few do. Some pension plans subtract the amount you receive from Social Security from your pension payments.

When you leave a job with a pension, keep a copy of the summary plan description that was in effect on your last day on the job, because this is the formula that will be used to determine your retirement payout. Make sure that you verify your vesting status and your spousal election. You should also regularly update your contact information so your former employer knows how to stay in touch with you and can reach you if there are any changes to the plan. Try to keep up with news about your former employer. If the firm merges with another or enters bankruptcy proceedings, another employer, an insurance company, or a government agency could inherit responsibility for the pension plan.

When you meet the age and vesting requirements, you will need to file a claim for your pension payments. Your plan administrator has ninety days to evaluate your claim, although the administrator can extend this to 180 days if there are special circumstances. If your claim is denied, you get at least sixty days to file an appeal. The plan then gets another sixty days to review the appeal, which they can extend for up to 120 days or until a committee or board meets to discuss the appeal.

Depending on how your pension is calculated, you may be able to increase your retirement payment by working more years or negotiating for a salary increase or overtime pay in years that will be factored into your payment. Conversely, you need to be careful about downshifting to a lower paid or part-time role before retiring completely. Earning a smaller salary during one of your final years of employment could decrease your pension payments.

Frozen Pension Plans

Getting a job with a pension plan doesn't necessarily mean you will continue to accrue benefits in the pension plan until you retire. Companies are allowed to stop future benefit accruals at any time, unless the pension agreement has been collectively bargained with a union. Employers freeze their traditional plans in a variety of different ways. Sometimes new employees are not allowed to join the plan, but existing workers can continue to accrue benefits in the plan. In other cases, the plan is frozen for all existing pension participants, and the benefit an employee will receive in retirement is calculated as of the day it was frozen. However, employers cannot take away pension benefits you have already earned.

Shutting new employees out of the pension plan often means that younger workers will never get to enjoy the level of retirement security of their older counterparts, even if they work the same number of years and earn a similar salary. Freezing the pension plan for all employees is often especially damaging to people within a few years of retirement who were counting on a specific pension payment to fund their retirement and have little time to devise a new strategy. Sometimes employers introduce or enhance a 401(k) plan when they freeze the traditional pension plan, but late-career employees often have little time for compounded investment growth to help propel them to a financially secure retirement.

For example, Jason is fifty and has been working at his current job for ten years. He would like to maintain this job until he retires at age sixty-five. Jason participates in a pension plan that will pay out 1.5 percent of his final salary for each year of service. However, Jason's company decided to freeze the pension plan this year. Due to his ten years of service, Jason will get 15 percent of his current $50,000 salary in retirement, or $7,500 per year in retirement.

Jason continues to work at the company until age sixty-five, and he receives annual raises that result in a final salary of $70,000. If the pension plan had not been frozen, his now twenty-five years of service would have entitled him to a pension payout of 37.5 percent of his final salary. The old pension system would have allowed him to qualify for pension payments of $26,250 annually in retirement. If he lives to be eighty-five, those pension payments would have been worth over half a million dollars.

Instead, Jason starts saving $3,000 per year in his 401(k) and gets $1,500 per year as an employer match. After fifteen years of earning 5 percent annual returns he has just under $100,000 in his 401(k). His twenty years of frozen pension payments, based on his salary at age fifty, are worth another $150,000. Between his frozen pension plan and late-life saving in a 401(k) plan, Jason comes out a quarter of a million dollars behind where he would have been with a pension alone. He also has the burden of managing his investments, paying taxes on the withdrawals, and making sure he doesn't spend down his savings too quickly.

Early Retirement and Buyout Offers

Financially struggling companies sometimes try to entice workers to leave with buyout or early retirement packages. A cash bonus or other incentive can be hard to resist, but it's important to think long term when evaluating what is being offered. The Older Workers Benefit Protection Act requires that workers over forty be given twenty-one days to consider a severance offer. Take some time to look at all the angles of early retirement.

The most straightforward way to evaluate an early retirement offer is to crunch the numbers. Compare the financial incentives of the buyout package to the salary and benefits you would receive in retirement if you stay at your job. If your pension is calculated based on your final salary, a one-time bonus isn't likely to be worth more than having a few higher-earning years factored into your pension.

Remember to factor health insurance coverage into your early retirement decision. If you're offered a buyout package before age sixty-five, you will need to pay for health insurance coverage from another source. Some early retirement packages include health insurance until you turn age sixty-five and qualify for Medicare. If health insurance isn't part of the deal, factor in how much it will cost to buy coverage through your state's health insurance exchange until age sixty-five.

If an entire department is being wiped out, there may not be much room to negotiate a better severance package. But if the company is being more selective with its early retirement packages, there might be some room to ask for more. The financial health of the company should play a role in your decision-making process. If the company doesn't get enough takers or natural attrition during the buyout process, there could be layoffs later without the cushion of extra cash.

If you're not ready to retire yet, consider how easy it will be for you to find another job. If your employer offers you a year's salary to leave and you can find another job within a month, the extra cash is a nice bonus. But if it takes you months or years to find a new position or the salary isn't comparable to your old job, you could come out worse off in retirement.

Several types of retirement benefits have penalties if you tap into them early. Your Social Security payments could be reduced if you retire early and didn't work for at least thirty-five years. Social Security payments are calculated based on the thirty-five years in which you earned the most. If you haven't worked for thirty-five years, zeros are averaged into your payment, which could reduce your monthly checks. Claiming benefits before full retirement age, or sixty-six for most baby boomers, will further reduce your payments. And if you need to use some of the funds in your IRA before age fifty-nine-and-a-half and 401(k) before age fifty-five, you will be forced to pay a 10 percent early withdrawal penalty on the distribution. Ideally, the early retirement package would provide enough compensation to avoid these two scenarios.

Pay close attention to the terms of the buyout offer. Make sure you are getting the compensation you are already owed, such as unused sick and vacation time or commissions or bonuses due to you. You might be asked not to work for a competitor or recruit customers or clients of your current employer, which could limit your job opportunities in the same field. The fine print might require you to give up your right to unemployment compensation or to sue the company for any grievances.

You might get a choice between taking your buyout as a lump sum or monthly payment. When deciding between the two, factor in the tax consequences. A large influx of cash can sometimes push you into a higher tax bracket, which means you will ultimately get to keep less of your cash benefit. If you have children in college, their eligibility for financial aid might also be affected.

Evaluating a Lump Sum Pension Payment

Vested pension participants are sometimes offered the option to take their benefits as a lump sum instead of monthly payments throughout retirement. When you get a lump sum offer, compare it to what your monthly payments would be worth over a twenty- or thirty-year retirement or an estimate of your life expectancy. For example, if you will get a pension payment of $1,500 per month between ages sixty-five and ninety, you can expect to receive $450,000 over your lifetime. This amount does not include the interest you could earn if you save or invest a portion of your payments. If the lump sum you are offered and the investment returns you expect to generate is less than the total of your pension payments over your life expectancy, you'll be better off holding on to the traditional pension plan.

Consider whether you want the responsibility of managing investments in retirement. When you have a traditional pension, a professional pension manager makes investment decisions on your behalf. You are guaranteed your payout, even if he or she makes poor decisions and loses money. A lump sum payment provides an opportunity to invest a significant sum of cash yourself. If you select appropriate investments, you will get to keep all of the gains. However, if you invest poorly, get tripped up by fees and penalties, or are unlucky enough to retire during a significant bear market, your retirement standard of living could suffer. Do-it-yourself investing comes with risks and potential rewards, and will likely require some effort and decision-making.

If you are married, your spouse's financial needs should also be taken into consideration. A pension might be payable to your spouse upon your death, which adds to the value of the traditional pension plan, especially if your spouse is likely to live a long life. Alternatively, your spouse could inherit what is left of the lump sum upon your death and would become responsible for investing and prudently managing that amount.

If you have significant health problems it can make sense to take the lump sum so you can use it to pay medical bills or pass some of the wealth on to heirs. However, if you have a spouse who will significantly outlive you, find out if he or she might prefer the pension payments.

Think about how much self-control you have when it comes to spending money. Pension payments are parceled out for you over your lifetime. Even if you spend it all as soon as you get it, you will get another check next month. Lump-sum pension payments need to be prudently managed to last the rest of your life, however long that might be.

When Pension Plans Fail

If your pension plan fails, you will probably still get payments in retirement. The Pension Benefit Guaranty Corporation, a government agency that pays out pension benefits up to certain annual limits if the plan ends, insures most traditional private-sector pension plans. When an insured plan runs out of money, reorganizes in bankruptcy, or files for liquidation, the PBGC assumes responsibility for payments to existing and future retirees. While you probably won't be able to continue to accrue new benefits, benefits you already earned at the time the plan ended will typically be paid out by the PBGC.

In fiscal year 2015 the PBGC paid $5.7 billion to over 800,000 retirees whose pension plans failed. The agency assumed responsibility for sixty-five new single-employer plans in 2015 and will pay out benefits to more than 25,000 additional people. The PBGC will eventually be responsible for paying benefits to 1.5 million people whose pension plans ended.

For plans that terminate in 2016, the PBGC insures payments of up to $60,136 annually, or about $5,011 per month for a sixty-five-year-old retiree. The PBGC insures small payments if you claim them before age sixty-five and larger payments if you begin receiving benefits at an older age. If you start payments at age fifty-five, the PBGC will only pay out up to $2,255 per month. The agency will insure as much as $8,319 per month if you begin payments at age seventy. Retirees can also elect to have benefits paid to a spouse after the retired worker's death, but the insured amount drops if you select this option. Joint annuities are insured up to $4,510 per month for people who claim at age sixty-five, $2,932 at age sixty, and $7,487 at age seventy. The maximum insured pension amount is adjusted each year to keep up with inflation, and is linked to Social Security cost-of-living adjustments.

If your pension payments are within the insured benefit amount, you will continue to receive the amount you have earned in retirement. If your pension was scheduled to be larger than the amount PBGC guarantees your payments could be reduced. However, the PBGC says most retirees continue to receive the amount they were promised in retirement. This guarantee does not apply to 401(k) plans, health benefits, vacation pay, life insurance, or severance payments. The pensions of small groups of professionals with fewer than twenty-six employees, religious groups, and the federal, state, and local governments are typically not insured by the PBGC.

The PBGC's revenue comes from insurance premiums paid by pension plan sponsors, recovered assets from failed pension plans, and investment income. The agency is not funded by taxes.

Find a Lost Pension Plan

If your former employer is bought or merges with another company, changes its name, moves to a new city, or goes out of business, it's possible to lose track of a pension plan you participated it. However, you could still be eligible for payments from your former company, a new firm that took over responsibility for the pension plan, an insurance company that is obligated to pay out annuity benefits, or the PBGC.

It sometimes takes research to locate an old pension plan. News reports about corporate bankruptcies and mergers are a good place to start. Former colleagues or a union associated with the plan might be able to provide information about what happened to the plan. Annual financial reports on federal form 5500 may help you to identify a contact person associated with the plan.

The PBGC maintains a database of unclaimed pensions that is searchable by name, company, and state. The agency lists approximately 38,000 people who are eligible for unclaimed pension payments. Over 2,000 former United Airlines employees have pension payments they have failed to claim, as do over 1,000 former employees of the mass-merchandise chain W.T. Grant. Nortel Networks, Circuit City Stores, and US Airways also have hundreds of former employees who haven't signed up for pension payments they are due. Thousands of residents of New York, Illinois, California, and Texas are missing out on pension payments they could sign up for. The PBGC says it has over $200 million in unclaimed pensions on its books, and individual benefits range from a few dollars to almost a million dollars.

The Social Security Administration sends a potential private pension benefit information notice to people who may be eligible for pensions when they sign up for Social Security. The Social Security Administration receives information about who might be eligible for pension payments from the Internal Revenue Service. This notice will typically contain information about the plan and an administrator you can contact to claim the benefits you are entitled to. A benefit statement, exit letter that confirms your participation in the plan, pay slips, or W-2 form can also help demonstrate your eligibility for pension payments.

The U.S. Administration on Aging manages a pension counseling and information program that helps older Americans to negotiate with former employers or pension plans for compensation due. The agency provides free legal counseling to older residents with pensions in thirty states. Services range from obtaining pension information from unresponsive retirement plan administrators to resolving disputes over benefit calculations. PensionHelp America, which was established by the nonprofit Pension Rights Center, can also help direct you to legal and technical assistance with your pension plan.

Pension Plans Transferred to an Insurance Company

Some companies convert their pension plans to an annuity paid by an insurance company. General Motors and Verizon arranged for Prudential Insurance Company to pay the pensions of some retirees beginning in 2012. If your pension is converted to an annuity at an insurance company when you are already receiving payments, they are likely to stay the same, although the insurance company might recalculate benefits when it takes over the plan.

However, when an insurance company assumes responsibility for pension payments, they are no longer insured by the Pension Benefit Guaranty Corporation. Instead, insurance company annuities are insured by State Guaranty Associations, and the protections offered vary by state. If the insurance company goes out of business, your pension will then be paid out up to your State Guaranty Association's limits. The National Organization of Life and Health Insurance Guaranty Associations (*www.nolhga.com*) provides links to State Guaranty Association websites, where you can look up how much of your annuity will be insured in the event the insurance company becomes insolvent.

Cash Balance Pension Plans

Some companies have converted their traditional pension plans into cash balance plans. These are defined benefit plans that have been amended to include some characteristics of 401(k) plans. Like traditional pension plans, the employer typically contributes to the cash balance plan on behalf of the employee. Investments are selected by the plan's investment manager, not the worker. And the value of the plan's assets does not directly impact the amount the worker will receive in retirement. Cash balance plans are insured by the Pension Benefit Guaranty Corporation up to annual limits, so vested participants will continue to receive payments in retirement if the plan fails. Retirees can choose to receive their payments spread out over their lifetime, including their spouse's lifetime, or select a lump sum.

However, employer contributions to cash balance plans are placed into hypothetical accounts with the worker's name on them. The participant's account is credited with an employer contribution and interest, which could have a fixed or variable rate. When a worker who is vested in the plan retires, the benefits are defined in terms of this account balance. For example, a retiree with an account balance of $100,000 at age sixty-five could choose to receive annuity payments based on that account balance. The Labor Department estimates that the value of this annuity could be $8,500 annually. However, the retiree and his or her spouse could also choose to receive a lump sum payment of the $100,000 account balance. In many cases this lump sum can be rolled over to an IRA or another employer's plan.

If you leave a job where you participated in a cash balance plan before you retire, you may be able to take at least a portion of your account balance with you. Unlike most other types of defined benefit plans, employees in cash balance plans vest in employer contributions after three years.

Watch Out for Pension Envy

If you do manage to score a job with a pension plan, you may not want to brag about it to your pensionless peers. Workers with 401(k) plans who didn't adequately fund them may be envious of your steady retirement payments that aren't subject to the whims of the stock market. It probably won't help to note that pension plans earned 0.7 percent higher investment returns than 401(k)s between 1990 and 2012, according to a Center for Retirement Research at Boston College analysis of the Labor Department's form 5500, largely due to the higher fees that are deducted from returns in 401(k) accounts.

You can try explaining how your pension is part of your compensation package or that you sacrificed a higher salary to enjoy this deferred compensation in retirement. Some employees also pay into their pension plans. At the very least, try not to look too gleeful at your retirement party if you're planning to invite people in their fifties and sixties who haven't saved anywhere near enough to retire comfortably. The best strategy is to admit how fortunate you are and express your sympathy that they can't have pensions too.

Five Ways the Pensionless Can Cope with Pension Envy

When you're barely scraping by in retirement, it's easy to feel jealous of someone who receives guaranteed monthly payments from their former employer. And plenty of people who are working past age sixty-five and scrambling to build a nest egg have felt envious of the government employee who claimed his pension payments at sixty. But resenting your more fortunate peers won't solve the problem. Here's how to get over your pension envy:

1. **Maximize the pension you will get from Social Security.**
   Almost no one will ever completely run out of money as long as he or she has Social Security payments coming in. Familiarize yourself with the strategies to maximize your benefit discussed in Step 1. Strategically maximizing your monthly payments by carefully deciding when to sign up for benefits and coordinating claiming decisions with your spouse can do a lot to improve your guaranteed retirement income. Delaying claiming your payments up until age seventy will result in higher monthly payments later on in retirement.

2. **Create your own pension.** If Social Security won't provide you with enough income to pay your monthly bills, you can set up a second stream of guaranteed payments. If you're willing to turn over a chunk of cash to an insurance company or charity, an immediate annuity or charitable gift annuity will allow you to receive a second stream of regular monthly payments. (See Step 6 for a more detailed discussion of annuities.)

3. **Find a job with a pension.** Traditional pension plans have not completely disappeared. Government jobs, a few large employers, and many unions continue to provide monthly payments to former employees. While traditional pension plans have requirements of as much as five to seven years of service to be fully vested, it is certainly possible to spend a decade at a company with a pension and set yourself up with a guaranteed source of retirement income. If it's important to you to receive monthly pension payments in retirement, factor that into your career decisions.

4. **Advocate for better retirement benefits.** The U.S. had a brief golden age of retirement security for a large proportion of the population. Not so long ago, in 1980, about 39 percent of the labor force had a traditional pension plan. While pension plan participation has been in decline for decades, it's certainly not impossible that pension plans could make a comeback. Pay attention to the political discussion about retirement benefits. Pensions were created so that long-term employees wouldn't have significant financial worries in retirement, and for the people who were eligible, it worked. It is within our control to provide a basic level of retirement security to our oldest residents.

5. **Make the best of the benefits you have.** Social Security will provide you with a basic amount of retirement income, and Medicare will prevent you from facing catastrophic medical bills. Maximizing these two benefits will prevent you from laps-

ing into poverty in old age. But you also need to build upon these government programs using 401(k)s and IRAs. These retirement accounts allow you to earn a tax break, capture investment gains, and perhaps gain employer contributions, all at the same time. It's particularly important to avoid fees and minimize taxes on your retirement savings, both while you are accumulating money in these accounts and drawing it down in retirement. The successful use of the retirement account system requires a commitment to regular saving, the savvy to artfully dodge a variety of penalties, and enough investment knowledge to capture the returns of the overall market. Investors willing to learn how to navigate our do-it-yourself retirement system will find ways to come out ahead.

Acknowledgments

I would like to thank my agent, Linda Konner, for taking on this project. My editors at Adams Media, Christine Dore and Peter Archer, contributed invaluable guidance. Jean Brandon provided endless encouragement. Craig Brandon contributed helpful suggestions at every step of the process.

I am appreciative of the support of my colleagues at *U.S. News & World Report*, especially Kim Castro, Katy Marquardt, and Kim Palmer. Thank you also to Tim Smart, Jim Bock, and the consumer advice team for giving me ten years to learn about retirement.

I could not have written this book without the support of Peter Anthony and Charlotte Anthony, to whom I dedicate this book. I would also like to thank Genevieve Wadas for teaching me everything I know about money.

About the Author

Emily Brandon is a senior editor at *U.S. News & World Report*, where she writes about retirement planning. She lives in the San Francisco Bay area with her husband and daughter.

INDEX